FLORIDA HOSPITAL *Healthcare & Leadership* MONOGRAPH SERIES

MONOGRAPH VOLUME VI

Building Bridges

A GUIDE TO OPTIMIZING PHYSICIAN–HOSPITAL RELATIONSHIPS

TED HAMILTON, MD, MBA

FLORIDA
HOSPITAL

Since 1908

FLORIDA HOSPITAL
HEALTHCARE
&LEADERSHIP
MONOGRAPH SERIES

BUILDING BRIDGES
Copyright © 2010 Ted Hamilton
Monograph Volume 6
Published by Florida Hospital
683 Winyah Drive, Orlando, Florida 32803

TO EXTEND *the* HEALTH *and* HEALING MINISTRY *of* CHRIST

GENERAL EDITOR	Todd Chobotar
EXTERNAL PEER REVIEW	Malcolm Herring, MD
	Brian Yanofchick, MD
	Joyce Portela, MHA
INTERNAL PEER REVIEW	Douglas L. Bechard, MD, FACP, CPE
	Randy Haffner, PhD, MBA
	Herdley Paolini, PhD
PROMOTION	Stephanie Lind, MBA
PRODUCTION	Lillian Boyd
COPY EDITOR	Barbara Trombitas
PHOTOGRAPHY	Spencer Freeman
COVER DESIGN	BONDesign
INTERIOR DESIGN	The Herman Lewis Design Syndicate

Cataloging-in-Publication Data for this monograph
is available from the Library of Congress
ISBN 13: 978-0-9820409-8-0
ISBN 10: 0-9820409-8-9

Printed in the United States of America
FP 10 9 8 7 6 5 4 3 2 1

For volume discounts please contact special sales at:
HealthProducts@FLHosp.org | 407-303-1929

For more resources on Whole Person Health please visit:
FloridaHospitalPublishing.com

CONTENTS

EDITOR'S INTRODUCTION

WHILE MANY HOSPITALS BELIEVE in the importance of having a physician well-being and engagement program, few know how to create or maintain one effectively. With his background as both a physician leader and hospital administrator Dr. Ted Hamilton is uniquely qualified to offer such guidance. In this important—even vital—monograph Dr. Hamilton:

- Digs beneath the surface of traditional physician satisfaction concepts to uncover the secrets contributing to deeper physician loyalty.

- Describes three indispensable elements that provide a solid foundation for physician-hospital relationships.

- Provides a four-step approach to optimizing first impressions when introducing new doctors to the hospital.

- Demystifies the concept of "wholeness" as it applies to patients and physicians.

- Provides a simple tool, based on Maslow's Hierarchy of Human Needs, to assess a hospital's approach to the well-being of staff physicians.

- Delineates a five-step approach to stimulate thinking about the growing cultural and religious diversity characterizing current-day medical staffs.

- Provides a rich resource of readily transferable templates, tools, and initiatives designed to jump-start efforts to strengthen engagement with doctors.

- Illuminates the peak level of human fulfillment as described by Maslow and its practical application to physicians.

- Provides a provocative glimpse at promising future directions in physician engagement.

If you're involved in healthcare or physician leadership at any level you may want to make this monograph "voluntary-mandatory" reading for your team. Because in these pages you will find help not only in relating more effectively to physicians, but in developing initiatives that will build healthier relationships between hospitals and medical staff that will ultimately improve patient care. And that's welcome news for us all.

Todd Chobotar, General Editor

FOREWORD

THE HEALTHCARE SYSTEM IN AMERICA is under pressure from all sides. Pressure creates stress for both physicians and hospitals that can put a strain on relationships. As Dr. Ted Hamilton points out in his timely monograph *Building Bridges*, physicians today face hurdles such as declining reimbursement, increasing workload, diminishing autonomy, encroaching bureaucracy, and liability concerns. These problems have robbed medical practice of much joy and in many cases reduced it to wearisome drudgery.

This unfortunate trend emerges at a time when physician leadership in hospitals has never been more crucial. Physician engagement is essential to providing quality care, ensuring patient safety, providing an outstanding experience for patients, and building healthy communities. Since doctors and hospitals are inevitably and inextricably bound together in the care of patients, it is imperative that hospitals help doctors find purpose, meaning, and fulfillment in life while working alongside the hospital to create a positive healing experience.

Instinctively we know hospitals and physicians are on the same team—though sometimes it may not feel like it. What can be done to create productive relationships between hospitals and physicians? Many things, including: good communication, mutual respect, ongoing support, recognition, and clearly defined objectives. But at the heart of a great relationship is a shared sense of mission. This point comes through clearly in *Building Bridges*.

In this monograph Dr. Hamilton does a remarkable job of sharing stories of Adventist Health System and their journey toward building bridges between hospitals and doctors. I particularly appreciate the way Dr. Hamilton details both the systematic (foundational) groundwork that must be laid, as well as outlining many programmatic (enrichment) elements that can be added.

This is a valuable publication I believe will be of great interest to the leadership of mission-focused healthcare organizations and their physician partners.

Harold G. Koenig, MD, MHSc

Director, Center for Spirituality, Theology and Health

Professor of Psychiatry & Behavioral Sciences

Associate Professor of Medicine, Duke University Medical Center

Author of *The Healing Power of Faith* and *Medicine, Religion, and Health*

"THERE'S A DIFFERENCE HERE"

"THERE'S A DIFFERENCE HERE." Krishna Das, MD, is a gynecologist-obstetrician who delivers babies and cares for women in the Smoky Mountains of western North Carolina. She partners with two other physicians in a thriving legacy practice that first opened its doors over two generations ago. Just three years ago, the practice moved, "lock, stock, and barrel," to a new location across town. Dr. Das admits that it was a "mammoth undertaking," a huge logistical challenge. But this move involved much more than checklists, timelines, details, and minutiae.

On the surface, it may have seemed like straightforward, good, logical business strategy. Park Ridge Hospital, a member institution of Adventist Health System, was opening a state-of-the-art Women's Center that would make it the "best-of-class" facility in its service area. Dr. Das' group was invited to become an integral part of making the Park Ridge Women's Center a market leader. It was tempting, but difficult. The practice had been loyal to a competing hospital for more than fifty years. This move would mean severing this long-term, established relationship. Would people understand? Would patients stay with the practice or seek out other options? How would the community respond? What were the financial implications?

The partners disagreed—vigorously. They analyzed known risks and potential benefits. They consulted experts. They weighed the pros and cons. Finally, they reached a decision—unanimous, albeit with varying degrees of enthusiasm—to move to Park Ridge.

Two weeks after settling into their new location, Dr. Das commented, "There's a difference here. I don't know quite how to explain it, but it's really neat. The hospital's mission is evident in the way people treat each other." Her partner's comment was a bit more explicit, "Shoot, it's hard to cuss somebody out with Jesus looking over your shoulder."

This colorful remark reflects a humorous and friendly perspective on what Adventist Health System (AHS) believes to be its fundamental defining difference within healthcare—its mission — "Extending the healing ministry of Christ." This mission statement is an expression of AHS's reason-to-be in the business of healthcare; this mission informs its strategies, drives its decisions, infuses its policies and procedures, infiltrates its operations, and enriches its relationships.

The practical application of this mission pervades the organization in a manner that attracts employees who are drawn to a faith-based, mission-focused culture and environment. Patients and families not infrequently echo Dr. Das' words, "There's a difference here." That difference is featured in statuary and artwork, "Jesus looking over your shoulder", but is more intimately expressed in the faithful, caring practices of employees and staff.

Adventist Health System aspires to extend the healing ministry of Christ comprehensively and pervasively, without imposition or offense, to everyone within its sphere of influence—patients and their families, employees and staff, volunteers, vendors, visitors—and doctors—the subject of this publication.

Adventist Health System's vision for the future anticipates that, "A high majority of revenues are from highly aligned physicians yielding superior quality, safety, and financial returns." This requires business relationships with physicians to be mutually beneficial; medical staff structures support a partnership in safety and quality; and a collaborative effort is undertaken to create a healing experience for physicians and patients alike. This vision requires new ways of communicating, interacting, and engaging with physicians toward accomplishing this mission.

I address this challenge in the pages that follow. The philosophy, concepts, and initiatives described here are grounded in the faith-based mission and culture of Adventist Health System. While the material is likely to be most compelling and applicable to leaders of faith-based healthcare organizations, the ultimate intent of contributing to the fundamental well-being of doctors and engaging doctors more effectively with the mission of the hospital should be of interest to any and all hospital executives and physician leaders who wish to pursue richer and more productive relationships with physicians. It begins by developing a rationale for addressing the well-being of doctors and strengthening physician relationships with the hospital and proceeds to provide practical examples and detailed resources to implement initiatives designed to contribute to this end.

PHYSICIAN WELL-BEING & ENGAGEMENT

"I HAVE THE BEST JOB IN THE WORLD. All I have to do is go from room to room, see beautiful babies and sweet mommas, get hugs and kisses, and be paid well for it."

Those are the words of my friend and mentor, Jack Facundus, who practiced pediatrics in Orlando, Florida, for thirty-three years. He began his medical career as an emergency physician, but soon discovered that his real love was caring for babies and children. Dr. Jack, as his little patients called him, never lost the joy of walking from exam room to exam room in his stocking feet and lavishing loving care on each and every patient.

Dr. Jack was not a dewy-eyed romanticist. He did not view life through rose-colored glasses. He often railed on the economic inequities of medical practice; he was not reluctant to criticize encroaching bureaucracy with its burdensome regulations; and he was quick to come to the defense of patients shut out of the system for lack of money or access.

But Dr. Jack never lost the wonder of seeing babies and children and their "mommas," one after another. He never lost sight of the importance of walking them through the early years of nutrition and immunizations, minor and not-so-minor illnesses and injuries, growth and development, and finally helping them transition toward adulthood. He enjoyed financial success, but what Dr. Jack valued far more was the intangible, reciprocal sharing of appreciation, respect, and love between doctor and patient. Deep meaning and purpose characterized his practice from the day the doors first opened until he retired over three decades later.

My experience working with hundreds of physicians across this country over the past quarter century suggests the existence of a pervasive and growing sense of malaise, disenchantment with the practice of medicine, and dissatisfaction with personal and professional life. What brought satisfaction, richness, and joy to Dr. Jack's practice has been severely compromised for too many doctors by the daily drudgery of the business of medicine.

A nationwide physician survey conducted in 2006 by the American College of Physician Executives validates this assertion. Based on more than one thousand responses, researchers concluded, "Doctors are exhausted. They're burned out. The stress of their work is causing marital and family discord. And nearly 60 percent of physicians (participating in the survey) have considered leaving the practice of medicine behind."[1]

Healthcare professionals are now confronting a curious paradox. While medicine is becoming capable of doing more and more for patients, health care professionals are becoming less and less satisfied with their work.

Dan Sulmasy, OFM, MD[2]

Reasons for low morale among practicing physicians include declining reimbursement, increasing workload, loss of professional autonomy and respect, encroaching bureaucracy, and medical liability concerns.[3] It should come as no surprise that many physicians report significant fatigue, emotional burnout, compromised relationships, and depression as a result of these stresses and pressures.[4]

In response to life challenges that seem overwhelming, many physicians simply give up. According to an Associated Press release dated May 8, 2008, an estimated 300 to 400 doctors commit suicide each year. This means more doctors are lost to suicide each year than the average size of a graduating medical school class. Another source suggests that the suicide rate among male doctors is 40% higher than among men in general, and the rate among female doctors is worse yet at 130% higher than that among women in general.[6]

> Although there has been tremendous progress in our understanding of disease and in interventions to restore health, many physicians have lost sight of their personal well-being.
>
> TAIT D. SHANAFELT[5]

Fatigue, burnout, disillusionment, depression, fractured relationships, and sometimes death—these are well-documented, real-life issues for physicians. And from personal experience, we physicians are often more diligent at caring for others than we are at caring for ourselves. Too often, we diminish and downplay our own symptoms, overlook signs of compromised capacity, and too readily deny problems that may or may not be apparent to those around us. We are prone to self-diagnosis and self-treatment, reluctant to seek professional assessment in our own behalf. Whether from a sense of obligation or necessity, we continue to work, make rounds, and care for patients when it would perhaps be better for us, and for our patients, to preferentially seek care for ourselves.

It is a good and helpful thing for hospitals to take a benevolent interest in the well-being of doctors upon whom they depend for the care of patients. Physicians and hospitals are closely-bound, essential partners in the care of the ill and injured. It is in the best interest of hospitals to promote the well-being of physicians, those responsible for writing orders, performing procedures, and providing leadership in the clinical arena. And it is in the best interest of our patients for physicians and hospitals to be collaboratively engaged in a healing endeavor that extends to, and encompasses, our physician healers.

Considering these issues, Adventist Health System has undertaken a new corporate initiative to more effectively engage physicians with the mission of our organization. Adventist Health System is a large, faith-based, multi-state healthcare system, sponsored by the Seventh-day Adventist Church. The combined medical staffs of the more than forty hospitals within AHS today number around 10,000 physicians. Adventist Health System comprehends that realization of its ultimate goal—engaging physicians with the organizational mission—is intimately related to, and dependent upon, the personal and relational well-being of physicians. This understanding leads to the formulation of new questions and articulation of new challenges.

What is the proper role of a hospital relative to the well-being of staff physicians? Are such concerns more appropriately the province of the organized medical staff? Is it sufficient to meet obligatory requirements for standard credentialing and monitoring of designated physician responsibilities that are directly related to patient care, such as call, consultation, record-keeping, professionalism, and sobriety? How do hospitals assure physicians of the altruistic and benevolent intent of such an initiative? At what point do attempts to address personal physician issues become intrusive or offensive?

This monograph assumes a legitimate hospital role in actively promoting the well-being of staff physicians. But just what does that mean? How do we address it? What approaches and activities might doctors find reasonable, helpful and attractive? How might progress be measured?

We have come to understand this challenge as two-fold; to help physicians achieve a sense of satisfaction and fulfillment in life while caring for patients in a clinically excellent and spiritually sensitive manner.

The means to that end are not so clear. While there are a number of examples of worthwhile initiatives in hospitals around the country from which to learn, few comprehensive programs seek to relate to physicians in this fundamental manner. It is clear that this involves something broader and deeper than mere physician satisfaction as traditionally described and assessed.

It goes without saying that it is essential to maintain reliable hospital structures and processes upon which physicians depend for efficient, effective, safe, high quality clinical care. Nursing quality, laboratory and imaging services, medical, surgical, emergency, and critical care programs, administrative functions, including admitting and discharge, transportation, medical records and billing, and the list goes on—all must work toward improving care for patients by facilitating the work of physicians.

> Forming relationships that center around shared purpose and values will lay the foundation for excellence and sustainability while restoring a sense of meaning, pride, and joy to the healthcare professions.[7]
>
> JOSEPH S. BUJAK, MD, VICE PRESIDENT OF MEDICAL AFFAIRS
> KOOTENAI MEDICAL CENTER, COEUR D'ALENE, IDAHO

But the challenge to support well-being is different. It requires thinking about medical staff development and physician relations in what is perhaps a new and different way. This approach is about more than providing an outstanding workshop with the best facilities and state-of-the-art equipment; more than having cordial relations with the organized medical staff; and more than achieving productive working relationships through skilled contracting and business development, although it includes elements of each.

This effort, Physician Well-Being & Engagement, is about connecting with physicians and supporting physicians at a personal level, at the level of emotion and spirit, heart and soul. It is about building professional, familial, and collegial relationships on a foundation of trust and fostering clear, honest, open communication, collaboration, and teamwork. To the degree that these goals are successfully attained, it is our belief that the outcomes will be evident in healthy physician-staff relationships and in a healing experience for patients in our hospitals and clinics. For Adventist Health System, this reflects an expression and extension of mission.

IT ALL BEGINS WITH MISSION

THE MISSION OF ADVENTIST HEALTH SYSTEM, briefly stated, is *Extending the Healing Ministry of Christ to the People and Communities We Serve.*

This Mission is reflected in a multitude of ways each day as patients experience relief from pain, recovery from illness, and comfort in their distress through the compassionate care of dedicated professionals in AHS hospitals and clinics. This mission of healing extends not only to patients, but to our caregivers, staff, employees, volunteers, and to the communities for whom we provide health care.

While the stated emphasis is clearly and directly related to the mission of AHS, these principles are particularly pertinent and relevant to other faith-based, mission-focused hospitals and healthcare systems. However there are also readily applicable to service-oriented, community-based healthcare organizations, and have relevance to any healthcare organization that is interested in more productive physician relationships.

> To be truly a physician…is to be committed to a noble ideal.
> EDMUND PELLEGRINO, MD[8]

The AHS Mission may be understood as four components—Calling, Culture, Community, and Care.

Calling: This mission implies that the care of the suffering is best conceived as something more than a good job, an exciting opportunity, a challenging career, or a distinguished professional endeavor. In the book *Called & Chosen*, Zeni Fox reflects on "an awareness of being called by God."[9] Regardless of one's religious persuasion, this awareness of a deep, indwelling commitment to a transcendent calling characterizes the most effective and best-loved healers.

While this concept is perhaps most familiar to those who embrace a religious belief or spiritual persuasion, it is also clearly reflected in the commonly heard phrase, "I just want to help people—this is why I went into medicine in the first place." Reviving an awareness of this stated purpose and sustaining a sense of meaning in the practice of medicine is elemental to a broad comprehension of calling.

Culture: To say that Adventist Health System is a faith-based organization is not only an indication of the origin and governance of our company, it is a reflection of the way people live and practice in the hospital. Adventist Health System believes, as do some 80% of Americans, according to a recent poll in *Time Magazine*[10], that faith and prayer are efficacious to the healing process. Many people, patients, employees, and others, but most particularly people of faith, are drawn to AHS hospitals as places where belief and prayer are part of the everyday culture of care.

A couple of years ago, I was admitted to an AHS hospital for a surgical procedure that required an overnight stay. My nurse was a young woman who had moved with her family to Florida from Canada within the past two years. When I asked her why she had chosen to work for this hospital, she responded, "My husband did online research and we were attracted to the mission of this hospital. That's why I'm here."

Culture involves much more than spiritual or religious beliefs and practices. It encompasses diversity, economic considerations, and ways of living and working. It influences and informs how people treat each other, how we communicate and address problems, and how we hold each other accountable. The challenge is to discover how to accommodate cultural differences while embracing a common mission.

Community: Adventist Health System holds inviolable two trusts. One is to honor and sustain the legacy and heritage of its sponsor, the Seventh-day Adventist Church, through loyalty to the ministry of health, healing, and hope envisioned by its founders. The other is to earn, maintain, and reciprocate the trust of the communities served by AHS hospitals through excellence in healthcare service and civic partnership.

Care: This mission calls for the highest attainable standards of performance in healthcare delivery, clinical quality, patient safety, and service experience. Beyond that, AHS believes that through the hands of medical professionals serving in its facilities, God's touch is extended in health, healing, and hope to humanity.

What are the implications for this particular understanding of mission in an increasingly diverse healthcare environment? While this concept reflects an overtly theistic understanding of the role of God in healing, AHS is not a homogeneous religious society. Its patients and caregivers come from a multitude of cultures and embrace a wide spectrum of religious worldviews and spiritual sensitivities.

Over the past forty years, the United States has become the most religiously diverse nation on earth. A recent article published by Farr Curlin, et al., comparing the religious affiliation of physicians to the United States population, graphically demonstrates this trend.[11]

RELIGIOUS AFFILIATION OF PHYSICIANS COMPARED WITH THE U.S. POPULATION			
Affiliation	**Physicians % (N)**	**U.S. Population* % (N)**	**P (x^2)**
Protestant	38.8 (427)	54.7 (800)	.00
Catholic	21.7 (244)	26.7 (370)	.01
Jewish	14.1 (181)	1.9 (26)	.00
None†	10.6 (117)	13.3 (198)	.06
Hindu	5.3 (53)	0.2 (1)	.00
Muslim	2.7 (33)	0.5 (5)	.00
Orthodox	2.2 (22)	0.5 (7)	.00
Mormon	1.7 (17)	0.4 (6)	.00
Buddhist	1.2 (13)	0.2 (3)	.01
Other	1.8 (18)	1.6 (21)	.70
Total	**100 (1125)**	**100 (1437)**	

* U.S. population estimate from 1998 General Social Survey data.
† For physicians, includes Atheist (2.0%), Agnostic (1.5%), and None (7.1%).

INTERFAITH CARE

In 2005, Dr. Mehul Dixit, a Pediatric Nephrologist, faced a daunting clinical challenge. Several children had been admitted to his service at Florida Hospital, an AHS facility, after becoming acutely ill following an experience playing with animals at a local petting zoo. The children were soon diagnosed with Hemolytic Uremic Syndrome, a potentially serious and sometimes fatal disease.

One child failed to respond to appropriate and aggressive clinical measures. Dr. Dixit had exhaustively reviewed the current medical literature, consulted experts around the world, and employed every therapeutic resource at his disposal. Still, the child's condition showed no signs of improvement.

Lying awake one night thinking about the child, Dr. Dixit recalled the words of a hospital executive, Bill Wilson, at the time of Dixit's orientation to the hospital. Mr. Wilson had said, "If you ever run into a situation where your back is against the wall and you don't know where to turn, come see me, and we'll pray about it."

Dr. Dixit took Mr. Wilson at his word. Together, they organized a brief time of group prayer on the pediatric unit, including the child's family, her nurses, her Hindu doctor and her Christian hospital administrator. Dr. Dixit says that it was about one hour later that they observed the first small flicker of improvement that eventuated, over the next several days, in the child's full and complete recovery.

"In our medical school training," Dr. Dixit said, "we were taught that we don't know everything in life. We want to serve people and heal them, and we understand that there is a power beyond what doctors can do to promote healing.

"The children that were affected put up the fight. Along with their families, they deserve the credit. Without their strength, no doctor can win the war.

"The prayer meeting strengthened the hopes of the staff and patients," Dixit added, "I treat, He cures."

If AHS is to fulfill its distinctive mission in this multicultural milieu, it is compelled to:

- Demonstrate integrity to its own unique identity.

- Communicate broadly for cultural understanding.

- Acknowledge and respect distinctive cultural differences.

- Mutually embrace elements of common purpose and practice.

- Build upon the deep spiritual wellspring that resides within each individual and unites all humanity.

While it is no simple matter to fulfill all of these objectives, it is essential that all are respected and pursued. The challenge is to translate mission into an inclusive, accessible vernacular; a compelling, engaging strategy; and a practical, workable program.

GETTING UNDERWAY

WHAT IS NOW TERMED Physician Well-Being & Engagement originated when Tom Werner, then President of Adventist Health System, and a small group of AHS senior leaders conceived of an opportunity to approach hospital-physician relationships in a non-traditional manner, from the perspective of mission. While the idea seemed intuitively to have merit, early concepts were more formative than substantive or specific.

> Start small.
>
> SISTER NANCY HOFFMAN, FORMER SENIOR VICE PRESIDENT
> DEPARTMENT OF MISSION & MINISTRY, CENTURA HEALTH

The initial task was to formulate and document an underlying philosophy and concepts for communication, dissemination, and discussion with hospital executives and physician leaders. What is it, really, that constitutes this initiative? What must be done to figure it out, give it substance, and make it practical and operational? How will it contribute to organizational culture, hospital operations, and the care of patients? How can the value of this initiative be assessed?

We began by meeting and talking with doctors, formally and informally, individually and in groups, over meals, and in weekend-long retreat settings. The discussions included ethnically and culturally diverse practitioners: primary care doctors and specialists; women and men; Hindu, Muslim, Jewish, and Christian; and self-employed and hospital-employed physicians.

We asked all of them the same questions:

- Do you perceive a need for what we are proposing to do?

- Do the issues that we've identified ring true to your own experience?

- Is this a legitimate arena for hospital involvement?

The answers were Yes, Yes, and Yes.

We discussed the challenge and asked for counsel and support. We learned that three relationships are of primary importance to doctors, regardless of specialty, race, gender, or religious persuasion. Those three relationships are physician-patient, physician-family, and physician-physician colleague. We came away from these early meetings persuaded that our efforts to address physician well-being and engagement must take fully into account these three distinctive relational priorities.

What Is This and Where Are We Headed?

What is this? The defining mission statement for this initiative drew from the existing corporate mission statement, adapted to reflect mission relative to physicians.

Mission: Extending the healing ministry of Christ to, and through, physicians

This wording is intended to convey that the mission extends not only to physicians in terms of their own personal and professional well-being, but also through physicians to the patients, for whose well-being we share responsibility. It must also extend to the staff who partner with us in this healing ministry. It is not intended to be exclusive or offensive relative to physicians who hold various worldviews, religious beliefs, and cultural prerogatives, but simply to communicate that the healing mission that drives the organization is inclusive of physicians.

Where are we headed? Creating a meaningful vision statement was challenging since it implies a description of a desired state, something not yet attained, something toward which to focus our thinking, energy, and efforts. Our vision statement is brief, comprised of three broad aims expressed in three succinct phrases that successively touch upon our aspirations for physicians, the organization, and the care of patients.

Vision: Physicians affiliated with Adventist Health System will:

1. *Find meaning and purpose in life.*

2. *Understand and value the mission of Adventist Health System.*

3. *Demonstrate wholeness in the care of patients.*

The first element of this vision is directed toward the concept of well-being and the second toward engagement, while the third reflects a desired outcome.

> Physicians, too, are hungry to rediscover meaning and purpose in their work, hungry to show up for something more than the money. [12]
> JOSEPH S. BUJAK, MD, VICE PRESIDENT OF MEDICAL AFFAIRS
> KOOTENAI MEDICAL CENTER, COEUR D'ALENE, IDAHO

The first is intended to address the previously-referenced, widespread sense of malaise and discouragement within the medical profession. An oft-heard assertion goes something like this, "Some physicians seem to have forgotten why they chose a medical career in the first place." This statement implies that an element of physician disillusionment with medical practice may be related to some loss of altruistic motivation for patient care. Today, physicians are faced with increasing pressure for efficiency and productivity combined with pervasive liability concerns. These and related influences may mitigate against opportunities for development and appreciation of positive human relationships that are intrinsic to the care of patients. These stress factors may compromise or diminish the meaningful, albeit intangible, personal and relational rewards attending the medical interaction for both patient and physician.

The first vision goal is to seek ways to assist physicians in achieving, or recovering, a sense of meaning, purpose, satisfaction, and fulfillment in life. A recent survey of physician satisfaction at Florida Hospital generated over seven hundred responses. As reported in *The Physician Executive* journal, the three most important factors that "make doctors more satisfied" are, in order of statistical significance, relationships with patients (easily number one), followed by a virtual tie between relationships with colleagues and relationships with their families. [13]

This research substantiates our early impressions derived from physician conversations and focus groups regarding the relational importance of patients, colleagues, and families, and highlights the challenge of creating an environment that assists physicians in building and strengthening these essential relationships.

The second element of our vision for Physician Well-Being & Engagement is that physicians understand and value the mission of Adventist Health System. This imposes an obligation on the part of hospital leaders to proactively familiarize physicians with the mission of the organization and with its implications for patient care and service to the community. Little can we expect physicians to engage with our mission if we neglect the opportunity to communicate our mission and demonstrate its practical influence on the culture of the hospital, the practice of patient care, and service to the community.

> The hospital's mission statement can be a sentence cobbled together by a committee and relegated to a dusty shelf. It may be that its physicians have never heard it or cannot remember it. It may be that the institution does not really live by the mission statement and, instead, creates a sort of institutional hypocrisy that destroys trust.
>
> MALCOLM HERRING, MD AND JON D. RAHMAN, MD [14]

For the purpose of corporate accountability, the AHS mission, *Extending the Healing Ministry of Christ*, is considered within three primary areas of emphasis, including Leadership & Culture, Environment of Care, and Community Health. Without going into great detail, the goal of AHS is to incorporate this mission into the very fabric of hospital operations and to measure performance across each element, incorporating metrics for patient and family, employee, and physician satisfaction; diversity/inclusivity; and community responsiveness, etc., as direct outcomes of mission accomplishment.

Mission accountabilities are reviewed formally each year and contribute to the assessment of executive performance. Mission is more than a framed statement on the wall, more than a high-sounding motto to be highlighted for Joint Commission—it is a guide for culture formation, an expectation for operational performance, and a standard for care-giving. A brief outline of AHS mission accountabilities is included as Resource A.

Since the influence of physicians on hospital culture and operations is profound and pervasive, it is essential that we approach the issue of physician engagement with serious intent. Many hospitals fail in this regard. A recent Gallup Organization survey of U.S. physicians revealed that only 10% of physicians are fully engaged with their hospital while 42% are actively disengaged. The study goes on to suggest a direct link between physician engagement, referral patterns, and financial performance. [15]

Wholeness in the Care of Patients

The third element of our vision is that physicians demonstrate wholeness in the care of patients. What is wholeness, and what does it mean to bring wholeness into the clinical encounter? In his book, *Ministryhealing*, Richard Rice notes, "However we define terms like 'health,' 'healing' and 'wholeness,' the expressions involve two central themes—complexity and brokenness." [16]

At a minimum, wholeness implies that humans are more than the sum of their body parts more than anatomic and physiologic curiosities more than components of brain, blood, and body, however marvelously arranged. Wholeness means that people are inherently complex, with abilities to reason and create, and with emotions, feelings, and aspirations that transcend mere biologic explanation. We are whole beings—body, mind, and soul.

Life experience informs us that human beings, however "whole", are subject to wear and tear; vulnerable to the outcomes of life choices and the vagaries of chance; and susceptible to illness, injury, and death. And when one part of the body is distressed, the whole is disturbed.

Physicians who are whole themselves, and who understand people as whole beings, know that treating a broken nose and multiple bruises is incomplete without addressing the possibility of underlying abuse; that assessing a patient for insomnia involves emotional and spiritual considerations; that diagnosing infantile failure to thrive means exploring environmental and parental issues in addition to nutritional causes.

> We teachers must demonstrate that we care for the patient, that we place the patient's needs above our own convenience and comfort, that we wear our authority and knowledge humbly, that we teach, explain, and are patient and sensitive.
>
> EDMUND D. PELLEGRINO, MD [17]

To practice wholeness in patient care means to sit down, use a patient's name and pronounce it correctly, look a patient in the eye, listen , touch, communicate with honesty and compassion, confirm understanding, answer questions and address expectations, and attend to a patient's needs and concerns as one human being to another.

The *Journal of Surgical Research* notes, "Surgeons should shake hands, use patient's first names, introduce themselves...make the patient a priority, and verify understanding." [18]

Wholeness for Physicians

The practice of wholeness in the care of patients requires whole physicians. This is a complex issue, not easily comprehended or addressed. The nature of medical education, training, and practice is characterized by expectations, pressures, and practices that tend to pull apart, break down, and splinter that which constitutes wholeness for physicians.

This fractionating phenomenon may be unapparent to physicians when the nearly impossible demands of professional life are perceived as ordinary and normal, an everyday experience, business as usual. Maslow's well-known hierarchy describes ascending levels of human need, including physiology, security, relationships, respect and esteem, and self-actualization. Although his theories are still debated, Maslow postulated that basic human needs must be satisfied before an individual is capable of addressing higher-level needs. Many physicians spend most of their waking hours in and around the hospital, often taking calls and caring for patients throughout the night and on weekends and holidays.

The chart on the opposite page reflects a graphic consideration of a hospital's role in addressing physician well-being and engagement as a practical application of Maslow's hierarchy of human needs. The concepts incorporated into the body of the pyramid are consistent with Maslow's original formulation. The words ascending the pyramid briefly describe and amplify these core concepts. The questions below the pyramid are intended to provoke candid assessment and creative thinking about a hospital's role in contributing to the experience of physicians in practical and meaningful ways.

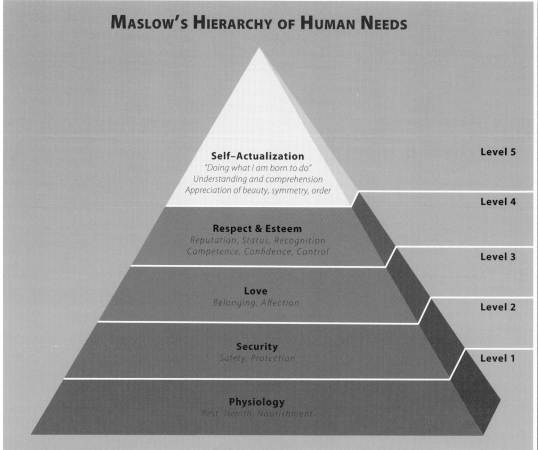

MASLOW'S HIERARCHY OF HUMAN NEEDS

Self–Actualization
"Doing what I am born to do"
Understanding and comprehension
Appreciation of beauty, symmetry, order

Level 5

Level 4

Respect & Esteem
Reputation, Status, Recognition
Competence, Confidence, Control

Level 3

Love
Belonging, Affection

Level 2

Security
Safety, Protection

Level 1

Physiology
Rest, Health, Nourishment

Self–Actualization
How can facilities be accessed for exercise and recreation?
How do we recognize personal & professional accomplishments?
How can opportunity be provided for expression of artistic abilities?
How do we express appreciation for a physician's support of the hospital?
How do we address the need for beauty "behind the scenes" in the hospital?

Respect & Esteem
How do we address issues of fragmentation and discontinuity in life?
How do we address physician expressions of pressure, burden, constraint?
How do we help physicians deal with issues of responsibility and authority?
How do we address physician perceptions of loss of respect and autonomy?

Love & Belonging
How can we support healthy and mutually rewarding
relationships with family, colleagues, patients, nurses, administrators?

Security
How do we address issues such as parking, safety, privacy, sleeping, exposure to natural light?

Physiology
When is food available? How about nights and weekends?
How can we optimize the use of "downtime" between cases?
How can the demands of on–call responsibilities be ameliorated?
What kinds of nourishment are available to physicians in our facility?
How can we provide increased opportunity for uninterrupted sleep?
Where is food available? Physician's lounge, cafeteria, nurse's station?

Many issues identified through analysis of these questions are neither expensive nor difficult to address, but they do require honest appraisal and intention to invest in positive change. To use a football analogy—as with blocking and tackling, this is not complicated, but it is critical to a successful effort. In our case, success means creating a culture of well-being for physicians.

Who is responsible for addressing these issues, and how might a hospital organize to address them?

BUILDING A BRIDGE TO PRODUCTIVE PHYSICIAN RELATIONSHIPS

WE BELIEVE THAT CURRENT AND FUTURE CHALLENGES facing the healthcare industry require creating new structures and strategies, new ways of organizing and providing care, and new ways of relating to each other and working together.

Our goal in this section is to describe foundational elements that are integral to building a Physician Well-Being & Engagement program, initiatives designed to contribute to the personal and professional well-being of physicians and to engage physicians with the fundamental mission of the hospital. The name of the program implies what we believe to be true—that in order to most effectively engage physicians with our mission, we must also be attentive to the primary needs of physicians to experience balance, purpose, and meaning in their lives.

It is difficult to distinguish with precision or clarity those initiatives that are primarily intended to address physician well-being from those directed more specifically toward physician engagement, and any attempt to separate the two may be perceived as somewhat arbitrary and artificial and not particularly productive. However, as we begin to describe and explore specific initiatives, a progression from well-being toward engagement will become apparent. While each influences the other, and is to some degree dependent upon the other, the focus of well-being is more on physician needs, while engagement has more to do with physicians in relationship with others.

Well-being encompasses concepts of health, fulfillment, contentment, and balance. Optimal well-being implies that basic life issues, such as nourishment, rest, safety, and physical and mental fitness are sufficiently addressed; personal and professional relationships are conducive to health; and knowledge and skills are utilized in a fulfilling manner.

Engagement is more externally focused, characterized by a high degree of identity with the mission of the organization, and incorporates relational concepts such as mutual appreciation, trust, respect, integrity, competence, and a commitment to service motivated by a sense of calling.

Well-being and engagement are different, but related. Well-being does not necessarily or inevitably lead to engagement, but well-being is indispensable preparation for engagement. Physician engagement is less likely to be realized, if not impossible to attain, in the absence of physician well-being.

The following illustration on page 23 highlights the sequence of initiatives necessary to construct a solid foundation for the bridge to productive physician relationships. The framework is comprised initially of systematic elements that are ongoing and critical to accomplishing subsequent objectives. Developing these basic foundational elements, layer upon layer, requires the intentional, collaborative effort of physician leaders and senior hospital executives, working together toward realization of a mutual goal—contributing to the well-being of physicians, and thereby to healthy hospitals and patient healing.

This illustration provides a graphic framework for understanding the intent and structure of this monograph. The goal is to bridge rough waters characterizing the healthcare industry and facilitate healthy and productive alliances between physicians and hospitals. Founded upon institutional mission, buttressed by systematic, foundational strategies, and supplemented by creative, enriching programs, Physician Well-Being & Engagement is designed to align hospitals and physicians in mutual commitment to healing ministry and service to communities.

The banners fluttering above the bridge indicate initiatives that may be more accurately described as programmatic, rather than systematic. Programmatic initiatives tend to be more project or event-oriented, episodic or periodic, intended to contribute towards accomplishing specific objectives or goals. Programmatic initiatives may be thought of as program enrichment, rather than program critical. This is not to discourage or diminish the importance of quality programmatic elements, but to emphasize the necessity for simultaneous development of the long-term, sustainable, systematic elements of a successful Physician Well-Being & Engagement endeavor.

This is not a trivial undertaking. It requires senior executive commitment to a persistent effort over the long haul. It is helpful to recall Sister Nancy Hoffman's wise counsel, "Start small." This is not something that can be accomplished as a short-term project assigned to a summer intern. There should be no anticipation of an overnight miracle. It requires patient, persistent effort and ongoing senior-level commitment. Constructing the first couple layers of the systematic foundation may require three to five years of consistent planning and implementation.

But it does not have to break the budget. Careful consideration of these systematic elements reveals that organizational will, dedicated work, and relationship building are more critical to success than large financial expenditures. Even for more cost-dependent initiatives, such as Physician Support Services, there are alternative ways of providing valuable services in an affordable manner.

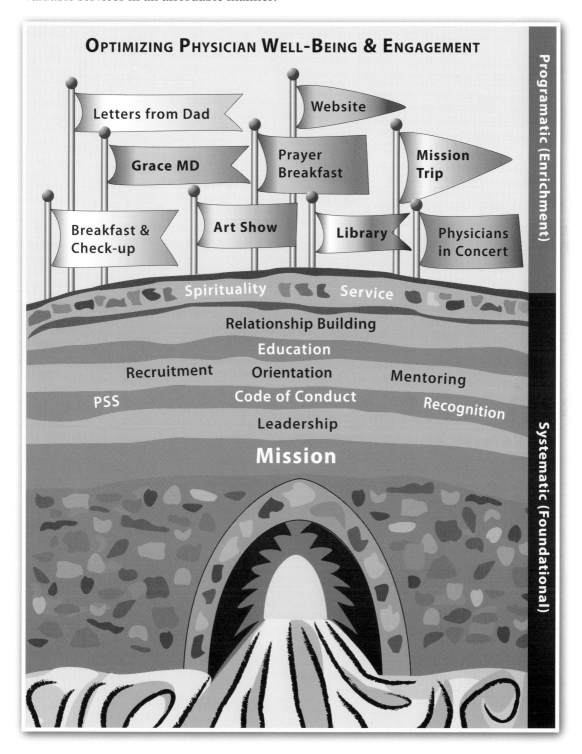

For the purposes of physician well-being and engagement, AHS makes no effort to differentiate between private, contracted, and employed physicians. Economic considerations notwithstanding, physicians are confronted with similar pressures, problems, and issues.

Nor is it necessary to contemplate a strategy that directly involves the entire medical staff. Research indicates that group dynamics and culture may be substantially influenced by as little as 5% of the group, one out of twenty, who are committed to moving in a certain direction. For example, consider a hospital with a total medical staff of three hundred doctors, two hundred of whom are considered "active staff," investing the major portion of their practice in this hospital. In this example, as few as ten motivated, supportive physicians have the capacity and influence to move an initiative forward. Bringing these key physicians to the table, introducing them to the concept, and engaging their participation is the theme of the next section.

Leadership: Since the active participation of physician leaders is crucial to the development of a successful program, the initial task of senior executive leadership is to identify doctors on the medical staff who are innately drawn to the mission and vision of the institution—doctors who feel a calling to the care of the sick and injured that transcends bare clinical considerations; seasoned, respected doctors who have a sense of responsibility for the well-being of their colleagues and indeed of everyone caring for patients in the hospital.

How can these physicians be identified? While it is likely that a number of physicians who have assumed positions of formal leadership for clinical programs or as part of the organized medical staff structure will have an interest and aptitude for becoming involved with this endeavor, it is important to look broadly among the doctors who are most active in the hospital and supportive of its mission. Describe the mission and vision of the program at medical executive committee, at general medical staff and departmental meetings, through medical staff communication vehicles, including newsletters and online resources, and invite discussion and participation. Interested doctors will respond.

Invite responding physicians, personally, one-on-one, eye-to-eye, to become engaged alongside hospital leadership, in this effort—an effort that should resonate with the core values, motives, and aspirations of each participating physician. The invitation itself is simple, practical, and straightforward—to lead, or participate in, a hospital committee that meets periodically to plan and implement programming dedicated to the well-being of staff physicians and their colleagues and families as an intentional expression of the hospital's mission.

This newly-formed Physician Well-Being & Engagement (PWE) Committee combines hospital and physician leadership. It functions most effectively as a formal hospital committee (hospital-initiated and sponsored); chaired by a carefully chosen physician leader; and consisting of several additional physicians, one or more senior hospital executives (Chief Executive Officer, Chief Medical Officer, or Chief Operating Officer), the medical staff administrator or liaison, and a hospital chaplain.

Minimal qualifications of a physician chosen to chair the PWE Committee include the following:

- Mature, seasoned doctor with several years experience on the medical staff.

- Current active practice, visible in the hospital.

- Respected and esteemed by the medical staff at large.

- Demonstrated loyalty to the hospital and support of its mission.

- Ability to communicate and collaborate with colleagues and hospital leadership.

Sample organizational documents are included at the end of this Monograph:

Resource B: PWE Committee Description & Organizational Chart
Resource C: Job Description, PWE Committee Chairperson
Resource D: Letter of Agreement, PWE Committee Chairperson

The CEO may choose to delegate direct participation on the PWE Committee to another senior executive; however, the success of the overall endeavor is critically dependent upon ongoing support of the CEO. A firm commitment to resource the PWE Committee's effort with necessary staff support and budget demonstrates executive resolve and support.

From a practical perspective, AHS consists of forty hospitals spread across ten states with ten thousand doctors on medical staffs, and since the corporate staff dedicated to PWE consists of two individuals, it is evident that the real work must take place at each local hospital and the corporate role consists of facilitation and support. Corporate responsibilities are, more specifically:

- Promote fundamental strategies related to physician well-being and engagement.

- Stimulate formation of a clinical culture that is faith-based and mission-oriented.

- Facilitate the development of mission-oriented physician leaders within AHS hospitals.

- Develop strategy for effective physician communication.

- Develop tools and resources with broad applicability across the system.

- Provide on-site consultation and facilitation.

- Establish corporate metrics for assessing physician well-being and engagement initiative.

It is now time to turn our attention to putting in place the systematic elements upon which to build a solid physician well-being and engagement program.

LAYING THE GROUNDWORK

THREE CORE ELEMENTS constitute a foundation for building a bridge to productive physician relationships. These include a professional code of conduct policy and process; a professional service for supporting physicians through counseling for life stresses, including specific mental and emotional health issues; and a system of recognition for physicians who demonstrate, in life and practice, values that are worthy of emulation.

Code of Conduct

There is now undisputed recognition that professional attitude and behavior is essential to providing clinical quality and safe patient care.

Unfortunately, as noted in the Joint Commission's July, 2008, Sentinel Event Alert, although most health care professionals "enter their chosen discipline for altruistic reasons and have a strong interest in caring for and helping other human beings...", nevertheless, "intimidating and disruptive behaviors in healthcare organizations are not rare." [19]

> Over a hundred years ago, George Rowe, a physician leader, wrote, "The average medical man is an educated gentleman, a delightful companion, a man of parts, and many such are our best friends. But doctors, when associated in corporate matters, are oftentimes too self-seeking. With an eye out for their profession, they are inclined to be aggressive, and naturally, under such conditions are not a gracious, peaceful, easily cooperative body of men."
>
> ASSOCIATION OF HOSPITAL SUPERINTENDENTS, 1902

The more things change, the more they remain the same. Today, the "average medical man" is no longer an accurate or adequate gender-descriptive term for the profession. Women comprise a significant, essential, and growing part of the medical profession. But Dr. Rowe's description of the behavior of doctors "under such conditions" strikes a currently familiar note.

A 2009 Doctor-Nurse Behavior Survey conducted by the American College of Physician Executives supports this assertion. In this survey, 97.4% of 2,100 nurse and doctor respondents reported that their healthcare organizations had experienced behavior problems with doctors and nurses. The most common problems reported may be loosely categorized as various types and degrees of verbal abuse, although other offenses, such as throwing objects, sexual harassment, and physical assault, were reported as well.[20]

> If a physician is disruptive or has personal problems, the hospital has a duty to intervene.
>
> THE FIFTH CIRCUIT COURT OF APPEALS

Effective January 1, 2009, the Joint Commission issued a Leadership Standard requiring hospitals to institute a policy and process for dealing with disruptive behavior in the hospital. This requirement establishes an expectation for standards of behavior conducive to good patient care.[21]

EP4: The hospital/organization has a code of conduct that defines acceptable and disruptive and inappropriate behaviors.

EP5: Leaders create and implement a process for managing disruptive and inappropriate behaviors.

While a well-designed code of conduct establishes and holds people accountable to certain standards of behavior, we believe that a faith-based, mission-focused hospital is called to a higher expectation than ordinarily described in code of conduct policies—a higher standard of civility, compassion, collegiality, and caring. Our aspiration is to transcend the skeletal descriptions of a non-disruptive workplace and transform our hospitals into true sanctuaries of healing.

In the mid-to-late 1990s, the medical staff and administrative leaders of Florida Hospital established a Citizenship Policy, the precursor to today's Code of Conduct. Each new physician accepted to the medical staff was scheduled for an introductory interview with the Chief Medical Officer and, as part of the agenda, was briefly oriented to the Citizenship Policy with a printed description of significant expectations for professional behavior.

Our experience with the Citizenship Policy was consistent with the findings of the Physician Executive Survey reported above. Issues were dealt with promptly by physician leaders and in the majority of cases, a satisfactory resolution was realized. Confidential records were maintained to track repetitive or persistent problems.

About two years after institution of the Citizenship Policy, a nursing leader expressed her appreciation to one of the physician leaders responsible for authoring the policy. With tears of gratitude in her eyes, she said, "I wasn't sure this would work, but it is working, and it is making a difference in our hospital."

This is not to suggest that the citizenship process is a completed initiative. It requires persistent attention and unwavering commitment on the part of physician leaders and hospital executives to maintain an effective policy and program.

About this time, Donald Jernigan, then President of Florida Hospital, placed another challenge before the medical staff leadership. "The Citizenship Policy is a good thing," he said, "I am grateful that we have it and am impressed and pleased with the impact it is having on the culture of the hospital." He added, "However, I am wondering if we can do something to encourage doctors, to lift their shoulders, to be of help to doctors struggling to cope with a myriad of difficult issues related to their personal and professional lives."

What emerged in response to that challenge is a multi-faceted program that we call Physician Support Services.

Physician Support Services (PSS)

The essential and irreducible core of an effective Physician Support Service (PSS) program is providing professional services aimed at supporting the relational and mental health of physicians, including counseling and crisis intervention. Physician Support Service maintains certain features of a traditional Employee Assistance Program—services are anonymous, confidential, and the initial six sessions are provided free of charge.

Common problems include marital and family issues, anxiety, depression, and bipolar disease. External referrals may be arranged for physicians with problems requiring prolonged or specialized intervention.

> Even though I've done my best to hide it, I'm a little surprised nobody noticed my problem sooner. I've been pretty low for the past two weeks. It's hard to get up in the morning and harder yet to make it through the day. Sometimes I just have to get away for a few minutes to get my head together. I've even caught myself crying for no good reason. Have I thought about hurting myself? Yeah, I have.
>
> PHYSICIAN NAME WITHHELD

At the request of hospital or medical staff leadership, PSS often provides professional consultation to assist in the assessment, management, and disposition of cases of disruptive physician behavior.

Look, I'm not happy about this. I wouldn't be here at all if the Chief of Internal Medicine hadn't insisted. I'll admit I'm not the easiest person to deal with, but when it comes to the care of my patients, I refuse to compromise, and people just need to understand that. I will not tolerate incompetence and insubordination. I want my orders followed without exception, and if they're not, somebody is going to hear about it. And right away!

PHYSICIAN NAME WITHHELD

Ultimate success of a PSS program is highly dependent upon broad physician acceptance and establishing trusting relationships between professional counselors and physicians on the medical staff. This can be difficult to accomplish when introducing a new program, even a program intended to support doctors and contribute positively to patient care and hospital culture.

Almost two years into the PSS program, Herdley Paolini, Ph.D., a clinical psychologist, was recruited as Director of Physician Support Services. One of her initial requests of leadership was that each new doctor approved for medical staff privileges be scheduled for a get-acquainted interview in her office. This was neither intended nor structured as a "mental health assessment." She asked about their families, homes, and hopes and aspirations for the future. And she followed up, contacting them periodically to keep track of what was happening in their lives.

She made them aware of the resources of her office—available to them as needed for counseling and support. To normalize attention to one's health, balance, and relationship issues, programs such as the Annual Ski Trip, Physicians in Concert, regular CME lectures, small groups, etc., were developed and regularly offered. These provided a forum for discussion, building relationships and trust, and nurturing culture change.

Dr. Paolini describes her approach to PSS as embedded, relational, and preventive. In the early days, she attended rounds, observed surgery, and accompanied physicians on call. She left her office to engage the world of physicians, toward the end of understanding their lives and earning their respect. And she came away with a first-hand appreciation of the need for physicians to attend to their own health and relational needs.

What do I do now? I never anticipated I'd be here, at least not under these circumstances. It's true that your hospital has been after me for some time to relocate my practice here, but the time never seemed quite right— until my professional partnership fell apart and my wife asked for a divorce. So here I am, drove into town yesterday, starting work tomorrow, new city, new hospital. No family, no friends, no furniture, and no food in the apartment. Where do I turn?

PHYSICIAN NAME WITHHELD

Dr. Paolini's casual, unassuming yet intentional approach opened the doors to her office and gave the PSS program a much needed boost. The informal, get-acquainted interview with the PSS counselor for each new physician applicant to the medical staff proved instrumental in breaking down barriers and creating a welcome sense of safety and support when a need for interventional services was identified. Within less than two years, Dr. Paolini's office calendar was completely packed and recruitment was underway for a second full-time professional counselor to meet the growing demand for physician counseling services.

PSS soon expanded its portfolio to offer additional services, including marital and family counseling, professional seminars and retreats devoted to physician well-being (with CME credit), social activities (such as Physicians in Concert), and service opportunities (including international mission initiatives). To date, the lives of several hundred physicians, in addition to their families and associates, have been touched by Physician Support Services.

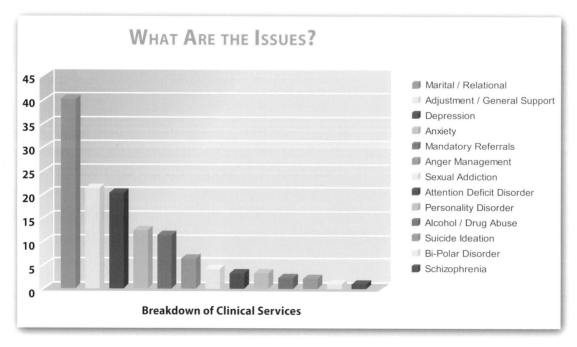

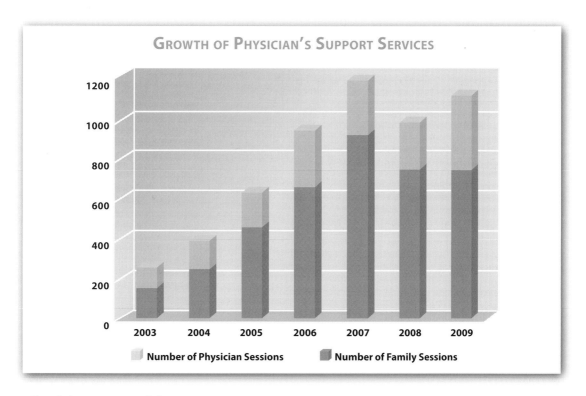

Physician Recognition

The underlying rationale for a physician recognition program is to honor physicians by promoting values and celebrating behaviors that are worthy of emulation. In addition to providing a deeply meaningful experience for physicians so honored, it gives the hospital an opportunity to highlight its core values before the entire medical staff and to say, in effect, "This is an example of the kind of caring service that we strive to provide for everyone."

The Florida Hospital Physician Recognition program is based on the core values of the institution— Integrity, Compassion, Balance, Excellence, Stewardship, and Teamwork.

Physician candidates are nominated by their peers, nursing staff, associates and administrators as representing and embodying these characteristics. The final selection of honorees is based on documented evidence of performance and assessment by medical staff leaders. To be optimally effective, there must be general acknowledgement by members of the medical staff of the integrity of the process and the credibility and authenticity of the honorees.

On the occasion of the annual medical staff banquet, recipients of each of these six awards are individually acknowledged and honored for their commitment to institutional values and patient care.

Recipients of Florida Hospital Medical Staff Awards for exemplifying institutional values had this to say:

Integrity

Integrity is a consistent adherence to a set of values—values learned from parents, partners, family, and faith. It is easy for a physician to become discouraged over liability, insurance, being "put upon" by the world. But we're here for the person-to-person relationship, and all the rest melts away.

HENRY HO, MD, ENT SURGEON

Compassion

The reason I became a doctor in the first place was not just to heal physically, but to take care of people with empathy. It's a privilege for me to bring relief and compassion when people need it most.

BETHANY BALLINGER, MD, EMERGENCY PHYSICIAN

Balance

Balance is meeting the needs of my patients and family with some down time for myself. It takes work, it's a learning process, but it's about being there for the people I care about.

STEVEN DUKES, MD, OBSTETRICIAN-GYNECOLOGIST

Excellence

Surgery is a team sport. Successful surgery is the result of an interactive team approach. The patient is at the center. Our job is to relentlessly, passionately, work to improve everything that touches the patient experience.

GEORGE PALMER, MD, CARDIOVASCULAR SURGEON

Stewardship

Using all the resources at my disposal, bringing a whole team of skilled and talented people together in multidisciplinary collaboration to achieve the best result for the benefit of my patient—that's stewardship.

JOSEPH BOYER, JR., MD, CARDIOTHORACIC SURGEON

Teamwork

No one knows it all. No one can do it all. Everyone is important. Everyone contributes to accomplishing one goal—providing the best care to each and every patient.

ERNEST PAGE II, MD, EMERGENCY PHYSICIAN

David Moorhead, MD, Florida Hospital Chief Medical Officer, insists that "physician recognition" is one component of the larger concept of "physician respect." He encourages hospital executives to consider questions such as:

- Do we proactively solicit the opinions of physicians on important issues?

- Do we value their counsel?

- Do we engage doctors as partners in critical initiatives?

- Do we express our appreciation in meaningful ways?

This is a complex issue, since the nature of healthcare economics often leads to market competition between physicians and hospitals, but is worthy of careful thought and consideration.

Resource E: Physician Recognition Award Documents, including Nominating Form, Awards Criteria, and Selection Process.

With this first layer of the systematic foundation in place, we take a step back to consider opportunities for establishing a healthy physician-hospital relationship from the very beginning—physician recruitment, orientation to the organization, and professional mentoring.

FIRST IMPRESSIONS

SINCE THERE IS ONLY ONE OPPORTUNITY to make a first impression, efforts to promote physician well-being and engagement should begin with the hospital's initial contact with any physician contemplating a relationship with the organization. A carefully planned, intentional program of physician recruitment, orientation, and mentoring has potential to pay rich relational dividends that will impact the institution for decades to come.

Recruitment: Physician recruitment is a complex process that involves community needs, professional politics, economic prospects and a host of related considerations. Of equal importance, and too often discounted or overlooked in the recruitment process, are mission considerations.

- Does this physician applicant understand and value our mission?

- Is this physician appreciative of the heritage and culture of the organization?

- Are the aspirations of this physician congruent with the goals of the hospital?

These are weighty questions, requiring more than superficial consideration. Ideally, the conversation that addresses these issues should be undertaken at the highest level of the organization. Brian Paradis, a senior AHS executive who has administrative responsibility for eight AHS hospitals, has directed that the interview of a physician applicant "cannot be delegated down." That is, if the facility CEO is unavailable to interview a physician applicant, the interview can only be "delegated up" the organizational chart, never down to a lower level of responsibility.

> The initial manner in which physicians and hospital leaders can foster communication is to make the opening of communication channels and the building of trust a high priority by using face-to-face communication…
>
> K. H. COHN [22]

This opening interview provides a critical opportunity to establish a trust relationship between physician and hospital and opens the door to meaningful ongoing dialogue. By the end of an effective get-acquainted interview, the hospital executive is no longer a nameless bureaucrat lodged in the C-suite of an ivory tower, and the physician is something more than a mechanistic revenue generator with a stethoscope and scalpel. Subsequent interactions begin with friendly smiles, warm handshakes, and, "How's the family?" before proceeding to discussion of business.

Dr. Joseph Bujak, Vice President of Medical Affairs at the Kootenai Medical Center in Coeur D'Alene, Idaho, states, "Trust is the foundation of meaningful and sustainable relationships." Writing in *Frontiers of Health Sciences Management*, he goes on to lament the lack of trust between physicians and administrators and attributes it to misperceptions and misunderstandings that arise due to failure of communication. He states unequivocally, "Trust develops in proportion to the frequency of meaningful interactions (and) all meaningful change occurs through conversation." [23]

Of course, this takes time. The old adage, "Pay me now or pay me later," applies. How much front-loaded and ongoing investment in face-to-face physician communication can a busy hospital executive afford? How much time can be carved out from other high-priority considerations—strategy, operations, finance, quality & safety, community relations—to focus on building relations with physicians, one doctor at a time? What is the cost-benefit ratio of casual conversation with a new doctor? This is as much a values judgment as it is a time-management or financial calculation. Each executive must find the right fit for each organization and set of circumstances. But it is clear that new physicians and hospital executive leaders (CEO, CFO, CNO, CMO) would do well to invest some time and effort, early on, to become acquainted with each other and better understand both the nature of the organization and the implications of their new relationship.

Orientation: Medical staff credentialing, followed by board consideration and approval, is a good and necessary process, intended to assure the qualifications and privileges of physician applicants to the medical staff. But the credentialing process, however well designed and executed, does little to introduce applicants to higher level expectations of medical staff membership. Obligations for call, consultation, and medical record completion are generally well understood and acknowledged. But considerations of mission, professional behavior, teamwork, communication, and collaboration are too often assumed and left unaddressed.

Rank-and-file hospital employees may be required to attend one or two days, or sometimes as much as a week, of intense orientation before undertaking new work responsibilities. Does it not make sense to invest a few hours of well-planned, efficient, productive orientation for new physicians, the doctors who will be responsible for the quality and safety of care of our patients, who will most significantly influence the culture and direction of the institution, potentially for many years to come?

A sample template for orientation of new physicians is included as Resource F. It begins with introductory interviews around the executive suite, with each senior executive contributing from specific areas of interest and expertise. It becomes progressively pragmatic as it proceeds through the medical staff office and hospital departments, service lines, and programs relevant to each physician's activities. The information communicated is important, but of equal or greater value is the opportunity to make acquaintances and initiate relationships with people whose function and expertise will contribute to the satisfaction and success of each new doctor.

Resource F: Physician Orientation Sample Template

Mentoring: Doctors trust doctors. Doctors listen to doctors. Doctors emulate doctors. Doctors mentor doctors. That's the way medicine is taught and learned.

In medical school and residency, this process is formal and intentional, built into the educational process. Upon entering practice, the same phenomenon holds true, but it is more subtle and nuanced. Doctors continue to teach and learn from each other, not only clinical skills and techniques, but professional customs and behaviors, ways of relating to patients, staff, colleagues, and others. Too often this process just happens in the routine course of daily work and practice, more by default than design, and the results are predictably mixed. Doctors emulate what seems to get the job done efficiently, what seems to be acceptable in the environment, what seems to work, what goes unchallenged.

In contrast, physician mentoring that is the product of intentional design and planning takes advantage of the experience and wisdom of successful and respected physicians to contribute to the professional formation of new, young, and less experienced doctors.

Physician mentoring may be accomplished as simply as identifying several mature, sage physicians who will commit to meeting one-on-one on a regular basis with each new member of the medical staff, including young physicians fresh out of training and those coming with years of experience. These informal face-to-face meetings, often scheduled over breakfast or lunch, provide a sounding board and solid perspective on how to achieve professional success in this new environment. Along the way, lasting friendships often develop that serve to enrich the lives of both participants.

> Good physicians...are honest and trustworthy and honor the trust placed in us.
> GUIDE TO GOOD MEDICAL PRACTICE USA [24]

Vascular surgeon Dr. Malcolm Herring and his colleagues at St. Vincent's Hospital in Indianapolis, Indiana, developed a formal, well-structured approach to mentoring physicians. A voluntary program, *Doc2Doc* matches mature physicians who have undergone a period of training as mentors with new physicians for a defined number of appointments over three to six months.

Doc2Doc is not professional coaching, counseling, or therapy. Physician mentors reach out to colleagues who are experiencing life change or stress and help them access resources to negotiate transition, achieve life balance, experience spiritual and emotional well-being, and discover meaning in work. In addition, St. Vincent's sponsors a training program for physicians who wish to develop or enhance their skills as mentors.

Education: "I have to tell you, I've attended this meeting for two full days, and I don't have any idea what it's about." The doctor who spoke these words is bright, sincere, kind...and honest. He approached me following the final plenary presentation of a two-day retreat on Physician Well-Being & Engagement. He, along with several other doctors from his hospital, had been invited by his CEO to this event. He went on to say that when he attends clinical meetings for his specialty, he knows what to expect and he's rarely surprised or confused by the content. In this case, I think he was making an argument for intentionality and for clarity, but beyond that, he seemed to be saying he experienced something unusual, something outside the ordinary fare of most medical meetings, and something difficult to fully comprehend or describe at first contact.

The principles, concepts, and techniques of Physician Well-Being & Engagement are not complicated, but neither are they part of the natural landscape of standard physician education and formation, nor even that of most healthcare executives. Efforts to establish a PWE program will require an educational process, first for hospital executives and physician leaders who have been identified as having an interest in this approach to professional development, and subsequently to larger groups of executives and physicians as the program gains momentum.

The educational process must accommodate physician schedules and priorities. We have found that one- to two-hour lectures or seminars, held over breakfast or dinner at an attractive location, are often well-received. For more extensive or in-depth training, a weekend conference or retreat may be more appropriate. The inclusion of spouses and families makes a weekend event more feasible and attractive for busy physicians.

Educational content will vary, depending upon the characteristics of the organization and the perceived needs of the physicians, but common themes include communication, collaboration, team-building, organizational culture, professional behavior, and, particularly in faith-based institutions, the relation of spirituality to health and the healing process. See Resource G for a partial list of periodic seminars sponsored by Florida Hospital over the past several years.

Resource G: List of Seminars 2005-2009

An increasingly popular element of our annual PWE retreat is "Table Talks." These talks literally occur at a round table, accommodating eight to twelve participants. They are informal, highly interactive, and designed to be both practical and engaging. In response to participant enthusiasm, we have doubled the amount of time devoted to table talks at the expense of reduced time for plenary sessions.

Availability of CME credit provides an attractive incentive to encourage physician attendance, but the logistics of obtaining CME approval are time consuming and somewhat tedious. Documentation required by the accrediting body, both pre- and post-event, requires a significant investment of time, energy, and staff support. A related consideration regarding CME credit has to do with Stark regulations. Charging physician attendees fair value related to costs for the event diminishes Stark concerns, but may have the undesirable effect of discouraging physician attendance.

Inclusion of physicians in planning and implementation assures their personal investment in the desired outcome of the educational event. We have tried to feature physicians as presenters for both plenary sessions and table talks. This lends authenticity to the process and stimulates interest and participation. A serendipitous benefit is the positive and rewarding relationships that often develop between physicians and staff during the process of planning and organizing an event.

At this point, it is prudent to ask, "How can I get the biggest bang for my buck? My hospital has limited staff and dollars. We are not in a position to implement a full-blown PWE program. How can we make a difference within our limited capacity?"

Data is currently unavailable to provide a definitive answer. It would be desirable to be able to make a case supported by hard data, including financial, physician satisfaction, patient experience, and clinical quality and safety. That will require additional experience and research. In the meantime, a subjective impression based on professional experience and intuition must suffice.

Of the elements making up the first layer of foundation of the bridge, Code of Conduct is now a Joint Commission leadership standard, and therefore must be addressed for accreditation purposes. Physician Support Services is more expensive and difficult to implement and impacts a limited number of physicians, but has significant potential impact on these doctors. Physician Recognition is relatively easy and inexpensive and has the added advantage of providing a visible platform for promoting organizational values.

All three elements comprising the second layer—physician recruitment, orientation, and mentoring— are inexpensive, but require senior executive commitment and participation to plan and execute. Where would I begin? Code of Conduct (both necessary and needed), physician orientation (get off to a good start with new docs), and physician recognition (acknowledge admirable performance), in that order. With those initiatives in place, I would explore a creative, affordable method to implement the physician support service concept.

Positive, healthy, productive physician-hospital relationships constitute both the goal and a facilitating strategy for physician well-being and engagement. We now consider strategies designed specifically to encourage relationship building.

BUILDING RELATIONSHIPS

IN ADDITION TO THE PHYSICIAN-PATIENT relationship, two primary relationships are unquestionably of fundamental importance to physician well-being—familial and collegial. Both have the potential to be a source of great strength and satisfaction, but both are vulnerable to the high-pressure stresses and demands of a busy medical career, and thereby have the potential to be destructive and disabling. Several initiatives are employed by hospitals within Adventist Health System to promote and build strong and meaningful relationships.

Physician CARES

A program created by Shawnee Mission Medical Center physicians and designed for physicians, *CARES* is an acronym for Compassion, Availability, Respect, Encouragement, and Safety. It means being available for physician colleagues for any reason, any time, any place. Physicians are prompted and reminded to send birthday cards, write thank you notes, and extend expressions of caring to colleagues in times of stress or loss.

Physician CARES also facilitates peer-to-peer support when needed and desired. Andrew Schwartz, MD, a cardiothoracic surgeon and co-creator of Physician CARES, stated, "Most physicians are lacking an environment in which they can find comfort, a listening ear and an individual who can relate to what is felt or being said...Who is better suited to understand the concerns, frustrations, sense of loss, and loneliness of a physician than another physician?"

CARES is instrumental in welcoming new physicians to the medical staff, orienting them to physician support services, facilitating their integration into the medical community, and promoting social events that help introduce colleagues to each other and to their families.

> I feel strongly that physicians can provide better patient care if they know each other on a more personal level.
>
> MARK BRADY, MD, ANESTHESIOLOGIST

Physician-Clergy Dialogue

This program also had its genesis at Shawnee Mission, when a small group of physicians and community clergy came together to plan a multidisciplinary conference dealing with ethical issues in health care. The experience of meeting and working together was sufficiently rewarding that they decided to meet periodically to discuss issues of mutual interest regarding the care of patients in the hospital. The idea spread and generated several additional small groups with a similar composition and purpose.

A typical Physician-Clergy Dialogue group involves four to six physicians and a like number of community clergy. Monthly meetings are usually organized around a meal, breakfast or lunch. While the dialogue is usually rather informal, it is helpful to have a prepared agenda to lend focus to the activity. Continuing Medical Education credit is given when a topic is planned and appropriately vetted, i.e., *Aging in America and Issues related to Elder Care; Death and Dying; Margin: Care of the Professional in a World of Diminishing Time.*

Physician-Clergy Dialogue is an interdisciplinary learning experience, but even more importantly, builds relational bridges of trust and support between the faith community, the community of medical professionals, and the hospital.

Meaning in Medicine

Under the inspirational leadership of Dr. Rachel Remen, the Institute for the Study of Health & Illness at Commonweal (ISHI) has developed several innovative programs that may be accessed online at *www.theheartofmedicine.org*. These include "Finding Meaning in Medicine," a program that affords physicians the opportunity to meet, in person or online, for the purpose of collegial dialogue.

Bringing physicians together in small groups averaging eight to twenty participants, Finding Meaning in Medicine provides a forum for thoughtful dialogue around issues of mutual interest. Commonly discussed topics include core values, such as integrity, courage, loyalty; the art of medicine, and the relation of the arts, literature, music, and drama to medicine. The subjects are intriguing and helpful, but perhaps the ultimate value of Finding Meaning in Medicine is associating with colleagues.

Porter Colleagues

Porter Adventist Hospital created "Porter Colleagues," a program to help physicians address the emotional and spiritual dimensions of medical practice, while also reflecting on what is most meaningful in their personal lives. Related to the larger Physician Well-Being structure, Porter Colleagues consists of functions that are time-efficient, include spouses when possible, and expand the influence of the program to as many of the medical staff as possible. These functions include:

- Yearly retreat with dual purpose of reflection and training.

- Monthly facilitated meetings.

- Affinity groups led by physicians.

- Weekly reflections, geared to physicians, that support the topics of the monthly facilitated meetings.

The goals of Porter Colleagues are as follows:

- Create a tool to allow for continually larger numbers of physicians to care for themselves and for other physicians in order to create a healthy physician community and hospital culture.

- Create a replicable program so that other facilities, particularly facilities without generous financial means, can benefit.

- Help physicians find or recover balance, purpose and meaning.

- Improve Patient care as measured by HCAHPS score.

- Fit the tool to efficiently meet the time demands of busy physicians.

- Fuel the hospital's strategic efforts.

A number of other creative initiatives designed to afford opportunities for the enhancement of collegial and family relationships have been implemented in AHS hospitals as part of the Physician Well-Being and Engagement initiative. While the preceding three initiatives are more systematic and ongoing, those that follow tend to be more programmatic and episodic. More information is available upon request, but a brief listing includes:

Letters from Dad

A small group of physicians gathers monthly at Park Ridge Hospital near Asheville, North Carolina, to write notes and letters to family members and friends, the people for whom they care most deeply and who have had a significant influence on their lives. In an age of instant and evanescent electronic communication, this commitment of pen and paper provides a substantive and meaningful reminder of events and relationships of most importance.

Grace MD

Grace MD is a CD containing personal stories told by seven physicians from Florida Hospital in Orlando in their own voices. These are stories of patient encounters, clinical successes and failures, and poignant moments, all experiences that remain in the mind and the heart of the listener. Narratives are our way of creating meaning and reality by processing the encounters of our lives. Grace MD provides a forum to hear one's heart and to identify with what is deeply human about the work of medicine. It helps physicians integrate their professional and personal lives and to get in touch with the spiritual part of daily work. The CD format makes it easy to listen to the stories in the car while driving to and from the office or hospital.

Communication Tools

A number of hospitals have periodic newsletters and some have created physician-oriented websites. This provides an opportunity to communicate content related to families, physician accomplishments, and service opportunities.

The medical staff lounge at Florida Hospital Waterman has a small library of books for leisure reading, borrowing, or taking "for keeps." The titles have been carefully chosen to reflect themes consistent with the mission, vision, and goals of physician engagement and well-being. A measure of success is the number of volumes that disappear from the shelf never to return. A representative list of volumes chosen for the library is included as Resource H.

Prayer Breakfast

Several locations have initiated periodic physician gatherings for inspiration and prayer over breakfast. Generally organized and led by physicians, these events tend to attract a small but deeply committed group of physicians who find deep satisfaction from this process.

Breakfast Check-Up

Park Ridge Hospital invited physicians to breakfast and asked them to come following an eight-hour fast. Before sitting down to a hearty meal, each physician participated in a health screening, including routine vital signs and a blood panel. This turned out to be hugely appreciated. Physicians remarked, "We do this for others every day of the week, but we never take the time to care for ourselves."

Physicians & the Arts

Art Show, Physicians in Concert, First Fridays, Family Picnic—the common idea behind each of these events is to provide an opportunity for physicians to change their scrubs for "real clothes" and to be seen as "real people,"; to showcase talents, skills, and interests outside of the hospital corridors; to meet the families and children of colleagues; to let down a carefully-sculpted professional guard; to relax, enjoy the moment, and have fun. These events have been consistently well-attended and much appreciated.

Physician Ski Trip

An Annual Ski Trip Event combined a family skiing holiday with the opportunity for CME credit at morning and evening seminars that included topics addressing the art of medicine—relationships, meaning, collegiality, balance, and integration of the personal and the professional.

GOING ABOVE AND BEYOND

IN SECTION THREE, we discussed Maslow's five levels of human need, including physiology, security, love and belonging, respect and esteem, and self-actualization. What is not so well-known is that several years following the publication of his seminal work, Maslow added an additional level, superseding even self-actualization as the pinnacle of human achievement. He called this final level self-transcendence.

Maslow's idea suggests that human fulfillment is optimally realized when we reach above and beyond the narrow confines of self-satisfaction and self-interest to acknowledge the existence and claims of a higher power and share the benefits of our own good fortune with others. In short, we transcend ourselves. This is a spiritual transformation, emanating from the heart and soul, evidenced through acts of beneficence, generosity, kindness, compassion, and love.

Acknowledging this unique "above and beyond" challenge, the Institute for Healthcare Improvement, an organization devoted to "leading the improvement of health care around the world" published a white paper entitled "Engaging Physicians in a Shared Quality Agenda." This document, available online at *www.IHI.org*, offers counsel for hospitals seeking to engage physicians more effectively. Many of the concepts and practical solutions addressed in this paper are equally applicable and pertinent to physician well-being and engagement. [26]

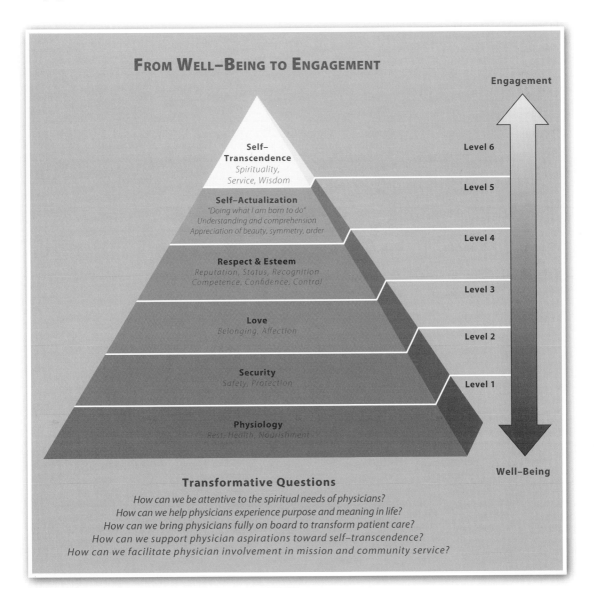

What inspires physicians to get involved, to become engaged at a higher and deeper level of service and spirituality? Sister Nancy Hoffman of the Sisters of Charity says, "Just ask them." It seems too simple, too direct, too bold. But Sister Nancy continues, "An invitation or request proffered honestly, openly, face-to-face, is very difficult to reject. You'll be surprised how many will just say yes, and give your proposal a try."

Service

Volunteering, donating time and skills to care for the poor and unfortunate; staffing community clinics; spending an occasional holiday devoted to foreign or domestic mission service; providing financial support to charitable causes; devoting some portion of regular office hours to the care of those unable to pay; supporting worthwhile community projects with energy, expertise, and resources; sublimating personal interests to the goals of patient safety and quality of care; all of these activities populate the uppermost tier of Maslow's hierarchy, the level of self-transcendence, the level most consistent with engagement with mission.

> It was my turn. My wife had previously gone to Africa on a mission to build homes a few years earlier. Several physician colleagues had traveled to perform surgery or deliver health care. Other friends had built schools and churches. I even know a veterinarian who used her skills to help animals on a mission trip.
>
> Now I was leaving for a week in Honduras with twenty-six compassionate men and women. I was worried about not understanding tropical diseases and being outside my hospital comfort zone. Over the next seven days, we were privileged to bring an element of hope, health, and healing to fifteen hundred grateful patients. One was a fourteen-month-old baby girl who weighed less than nine pounds. This starving child and her mother were brought to our mission base to be nourished and loved back to full health.
>
> We could not deliver fully comprehensive medical care to so many in such a short period of time, but their lives, and ours, were touched in a multitude of positive and meaningful ways.
>
> DR. LANNY WILSON, ADVENTIST MIDWEST HEALTH

Centura Health

Global Health Initiatives originated in 2006 when Centura Health initiated a partnership between several Adventist hospitals in Colorado and mission hospitals in Central and South America, Africa, and Asia. These partnerships include the following mission hospitals:

- Clinica Adventista Ana Stahl, Iquitos, Peru

- La Loma Luz Adventist Hospital, San Ignacio, Belize

- Mugonero Hospital, Ngoma, Rwanda

- Scheer Memorial Hospital, Banepa, Nepal

Global Health Initiatives was founded on the following principles:

1. Medical missions provide an opportunity for Centura Health physicians, nurses and other health professionals to provide humanitarian services in countries with tremendous healthcare needs.

2. Assistance given to mission hospitals involves a variety of endeavors, including providing medical equipment and supplies, continuing education for mission hospital staff, organizing limited building projects, and providing direct services to patients (both in-and out-patient). The end goal, though, is to strengthen the mission hospitals and build their capacity to serve their communities.

3. The partnerships that have been established are long-term relationships between Centura Health and the mission hospitals. Lasting change requires patience, time, and ongoing investment; therefore, a multiple-year approach is being pursued.

4. Medical mission projects seek to strengthen the alignment between physicians and hospital staff and with the healing ministry of Jesus Christ and the mission of Centura Health.

During the past four years, twenty-six medical mission teams, including more than one hundred physicians, traveled to the four partner hospitals. Nearly 15,000 patients have received services from Centura Health teams, and over $3 million in travel expenses, equipment, and cash has been donated to the projects.

> Physicians have grown inwardly focused in response to the complexity and unpredictability of their daily lives.
>
> T.R. BILLIAR[25]

OUR STORY
A COMPOSITE EXCERPT FROM VIDEO PRESENTATION

The mission of Centura Health, Extending the Healing Ministry of Jesus Christ to the people and communities we serve, is not just a local mission. We understand it as a global mission. Global Health Initiative gives doctors a wonderful opportunity to give back, to help people with the most profound need.

We see a whole different side of humanity, the poorest of the poor, with no access to medical care, lined up for hours to see a doctor. We have no technology to speak of, so we use our heads, our hands, and our hearts to make a diagnosis and administer a treatment. What we learn and experience in the mission enriches our practice back home.

It's a soulful experience. We're better human beings and better doctors for having done this. It puts us in touch with why we went into medicine in the beginning.

DOUGLAS DENNIS, MD, ORTHOPEDIC SURGERY
DEBRA GRADICK, MD, EMERGENCY MEDICINE
DAVE EHRENBERGER, MD, FAMILY PHYSICIAN
DAVID SCHNEIDER, MD, ORTHOPEDIC SURGERY

TED NING, MD, UROLOGY
TERESA HEBLE, MD, FAMILY PHYSICIAN
DAVID RAPHAEL, MD, ANESTHESIA
LINDA TETOR, MD, FAMILY PRACTICE

While a foreign mission trip may be a life-changing experience for patients and providers alike, it is not necessary to travel outside the United States to find opportunities to serve people who are desperately in need of medical care. Shepherd's Hope is a not-for-profit organization located in Orlando, Florida, with a mission to provide free acute medical services for people who are impoverished and uninsured. Today, some thirteen years after its inception, Shepherd's Hope provides 16,000 patient visits each year through the donated services of 3,000 volunteers, including some three hundred doctors and five hundred nurses. What follows is an account of my own experience at Shepard's Hope.

A Rewarding Experience

Here they are. My patients. Eight of them in all.

Adults, ages thirty-six to seventy.

Two men, six women.

Four of Hispanic heritage, two African American, two Caucasion.

Of the three who speak no English, two are fluent in Spanish, one speaks French Creole.

Four of them have come primarily because they have run out of their medicines. Prescription meds for elevated cholesterol, high blood pressure, diabetes (her blood sugar is 270 tonight). The one who needs thyroid replacement medication has been out of meds for three months and her skin and hair are dry and brittle.

They're not particular, they'll take what we can provide off the shelf from our limited formulary, or, failing that, they're grateful to receive discounted prescriptions that they can fill at the drug store...when they can come up with the money. Those are the easy ones. Pick up the generic medicine just down the hall or write a script. Good-bye. See you in two months.

Some take a bit more time.

The sixty-year-old grandmother who works everyday in a laundry... lifting, pulling, pushing...has sustained a painful injury to her rib cage. Is it bruised or broken? She leaves with a bottle of ibuprofen for pain and an order for X-rays of her chest and ribs.

In the next room is a thirty-six- year-old gentleman who is an eighteen-month sober alcoholic and recovered TB patient. He is referred to an ophthalmologist for his significantly blurred vision.

That leaves the bookends, the first and last patients I'll see this evening.

Behind the first door is a fifty-nine- year-old Caucasian male, moderately obese, high blood pressure, elevated blood sugar, complaining of recurrent tightness in his upper chest and neck. Our nurse does an EKG. There are abnormal ST segment changes in the lateral leads. Despite his initial reluctance, he's off to the nearest Emergency Department for immediate assessment. Behind the last door is a thirty-eight-year-old woman who's had diabetes most of her life. She works every day as a nursing assistant. But it is challenging to carry out her duties with her swollen foot. She removes her bandage to reveal a black and gangrenous large toe.

She needs immediate hospitalization and surgery to save her foot. But she won't go tonight...she has a tween-age child alone at home. She promises she'll go in tomorrow when she can arrange for child care.

That's it. We're done.

File the charts. Put away the equipment and supplies.

Turn off the lights. Lock the door.

It's just another night at the clinic.

Just another night at Shepherd's Hope.

TED HAMILTON, MD, FAMILY PHYSICIAN

Dr. Greg Zittel, a volunteer Ob-Gyn specialist, says, "There are times I drive to the volunteer clinic after putting in a long day and I ask myself, 'Why did I agree to do this?' But as soon I get started seeing patients, I feel better," he says with a smile. "It's a blessing and a privilege to do this work."

What is it that makes a volunteer clinic experience special from the physician's perspective? After all, we do the same kind of work all day long, one patient after another— history and physical, order tests, write prescriptions. And we often come to this work at the end of a long day, tired and worn out. But we rarely leave the clinic feeling fatigued; there is a sense of satisfaction that accompanies this work and imparts its own energy.

I think it has something to do with the patients, their need and their appreciation, and with the absence of bureaucracy and not stressing over finances, overhead, and productivity. For a recent presentation, I related stories of patients I had encountered, patients who entrusted me with their care. For me, it is these patients that make the volunteer clinic experience rewarding.

Spirituality

Last Monday, we were rushing a patient to the cath lab for an emergency procedure. Out of nowhere, Chaplain Vicki appeared. I assumed she was going to ask me how the patient was doing so she could update the family. I was surprised when she asked me how I was doing and if there was anything she could do for me. In all my experience as an anesthesiologist with its attendant stress, contending with critical, life-and-death situations, no one had ever asked how I was or if there was anything I needed.

Frankly, I always struggled a bit to put a hard, definable edge on what to me is a very soft topic. I now have first-hand experience how the 'soft around the edges' physician wellness concept can pay hard benefits to the physicians, even if it is something as simple as asking how someone is doing. That simple gesture was totally unique from anywhere I have ever worked or trained, and I view it as a nice value-added benefit of working in Adventist Health System.

DANIEL LEVINTHAL, MD, ANESTHESIOLOGY

Sometimes, as Dr. Levinthal's story aptly illustrates, it turns out that the hard stuff is the soft stuff and the soft stuff is the hard stuff. For centuries, medicine and spirituality were inseparably intertwined. Before the advent of the scientific revolution in the twentieth century, spiritual leaders often doubled as practitioners of the healing arts. In the Middle Ages, the church issued medical licenses and priests and nuns cared for the ill and injured.

But the advance of medical knowledge and clinical acumen in the twentieth-century United States led to a schism between the care of the body and the care of the soul, such that today, "spirituality may seem out of place in a field grounded in hard science."[27] This is somewhat counter-intuitive, since about three out of four Americans believe that faith is related to healing and would welcome a conversation about spiritual matters with their physicians.[28] A similar percentage of doctors believe in God and, in one survey, a majority (59%) of U.S. doctors said they believe in some sort of afterlife.[29]

It is important to make a distinction between religion and spirituality. Definitions and expressions of personal spirituality are numerous, variegated and multi-hued. Religion, on the other hand, while appearing in a multitude of varieties, lends itself more easily to definition and description, consisting as it commonly does, of belief in a transcendent deity, a moral code, a set of beliefs and practices, and a community of followers.

One author states that "spirituality is more individualistic and self-determined, whereas religion typically involves connections to a community with shared beliefs and rituals."[30] Another suggests that a "practical approach is to envision spirituality as addressing universal human questions and needs, and religion as providing specific (and often differing) answers to those questions, and ways of meeting those needs."[31]

Research demonstrates an association between religious beliefs and practices and lower suicide rates, less anxiety, substance abuse, and depression; greater well-being, hope, and optimism; more purpose and meaning in life; higher social support; and greater marital satisfaction.[32]

This sounds like good medicine—for physicians and patients. Our challenge, then, is to make this good medicine available to doctors and patients alike without imposing sectarian beliefs or offending the spiritual sensitivities of those who do not appreciate our point of view.

As Dan Sulmasy, OFM, MD, points out in his book, *The Healer's Calling*, this can be a difficult issue. "In a very pluralistic society like our own," he writes, "big questions arise about how and when to engage the question of God with patients."[33] Dr. Sulmasy goes on to discuss how various encounters might be managed between patients and doctors when either or both parties espouse or deny religious belief.

A growing number of U.S. medical schools are introducing spirituality in undergraduate medical education, familiarizing students with the underlying concepts and training them to address spiritual concerns with patients in the same manner that they review medications, allergies, and medical history.

In 2008, under the leadership of Dr. John Guarneri, then President of the Florida Hospital Medical Staff, the medical executive committee took unanimous action to formally create a Department of Healthcare & Spirituality. The goals of this department are:

- Educate and facilitate physician understanding on the spiritual aspects of patient care.

- Collaborate with the healthcare delivery team on the spiritual aspects of patient care, with emphasis and consultation from the pastoral care team.

- Collaborate and further establish relationships with faith communities and their leaders on the spiritual care of patients.

- Support and foster the spiritual life and well-being of physicians.

- Identify Florida Hospital's and national best practices and collect data to determine where evidence supports improved outcomes.

Sections of the Department of Healthcare & Spirituality have been established at all eight Florida Hospital campuses, with designated physician leaders and functioning committees. Dr. Guarneri continues to serve as immediate past president of the medical staff and devotes 40% of his professional time to organizing and promoting activities of this new medical staff department.

Resource I: Department of Healthcare & Spirituality

A GRAND VISION

WHERE DO WE GO FROM HERE? In pursuing the mission and goals of Physician Well-Being & Engagement, we continually seek new ways of relating to, and collaborating with, physicians. Along the way, we must evaluate these methods and initiatives and begin to understand how and why some work and others fail; it becomes essential to assess our progress through careful scrutiny and scholarly research and to measure, document, and communicate the results of our work.

Exposing our work to the broader community enriches the process and provides a stimulus for further growth and achievement.

Adventist Health System is considering a uniform, system-wide Physician Satisfaction Survey. Administered under the auspices of a national vendor, this standardized survey will provide both internal and external norms for comparison. In addition to routine questions related to hospital quality and services, we are considering including several statements assessing commitment to mission, institutional loyalty, and physician well-being, such as, "This organization cares about my personal well-being," and, "I have a colleague or mentor whose counsel I trust."

Under the leadership of Florida Hospital Center for Health Futures, a comprehensive self-assessment tool has been developed for physicians to assess their own health and well-being. The Physician Well-Being Self-Assessment Tool (PWSAT) seeks to better understand physicians' challenges, support and improve physician well-being, and improve patient safety and quality. For the purposes of this survey tool, physician well-being was defined as the intentional cultivation of an optimal personal and professional experience by and for physicians. The Physician Well-Being Self-Assessment Tool measures four domains of experience in which well-being may be optimized: bio-physical, psycho-emotional, socio-relational, and religion-spiritual. This tool is now used annually in our residency programs, has been adopted by other hospitals, and is being adapted for use in medical schools.

Inside the Mind of a Physician is a monograph, authored by Herdley Paolini, Ph.D., Director of Florida Hospital Physician Support Services. This publication, in the words of the subtitle, sets out to illuminate "the mystery of how doctors think, what they feel, and why they do the things they do." Dr. Paolini draws upon eight years of experience meeting and counseling with physicians, understanding their training and formation, the nature of their struggles and challenges, and the manner in which their thinking affects behavior. This work provides valuable insight for all who work with physicians, desire to understand them better, and strive to work with them more effectively.

While most AHS hospitals have initiated a Physician Well-Being & Engagement program, the degree of accomplishment varies—some initiatives are thriving, while others have faltered. It is encouraging to see cross-fertilization emerging between hospitals as successful programs share what they have learned and others follow their lead.

A useful tool for assessing institutional progress in a qualitative manner is the development of a "Mind Map." This technique or process creates a visual representation of existing initiatives, challenges, and opportunities. Color-coding can offer a quick visual representation of the status of identified issues if you choose.

Are our efforts making a difference? While our data remains mostly anecdotal to date, the stories of physicians whose lives have been touched and changed by this effort are accumulating from all parts of the company. Attendance at our annual convention doubled since our initial meeting in 2006. More CEOs and physicians are taking responsibility for PWE leadership. We believe a strong foundation has been built and we remain convinced of the strategic value and inherent rightness of the course we are pursuing.

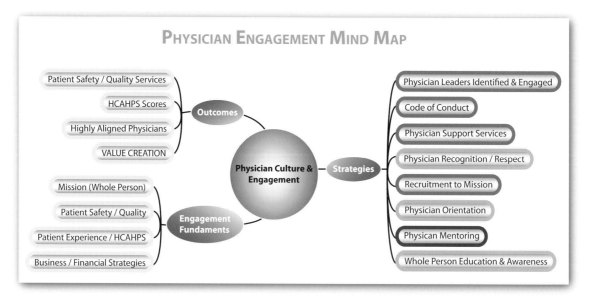

How do we move Physician Well-Being & Engagement forward? When asked that question, AHS Chief Information Officer, Dr. Phil Smith, responded, "Find a fire and pour fuel on it." That's what we try to do. Through communication, motivation, promotion, education, facilitation and support, developing tools and resources, encouragement, and persistence, we try to bring the flickering flame of good ideas to full blaze.

Our vision has evolved and grown along with our understanding of the Physician Well-Being & Engagement Initiative. The current expression of our vision is stated below. If it seems to lack specificity and definition, it is because we are figuring it out as we go. It is, after all, a vision, not yet a reality. While we believe this to be an aggressive vision, we also believe it to be attainable and essential to our ongoing success as a faith-based, mission-focused healthcare organization.

AHS Vision: Physician Well-Being & Engagement

AHS hospitals and physicians are aligned in mutual commitment to healing ministry and service to our communities.

- AHS Mission, Vision, and Values infuse hospital-medical staff relationships, including recruitment, application process, orientation, mentoring, recognition, medical leadership development, and contracts.

- Physician Well-Being & Engagement is facilitated through engagement of senior executive leadership and appropriate investments of money and staff. Initiatives designed to enrich collegial and familial relationships, including access to professional counseling services, are deployed in all markets.

- Wholeness in patient care based upon four dimensions of healing, including relationships to the Transcendent, self, others, and the environment, is broadly promoted through physician awareness, education, and modeling.

- Clinical teamwork is facilitated by mutual appreciation and effective communication and collaboration between physicians and staff.

- Physician Well-Being & Engagement has achieved sustainable influence and prominence through effective communication, research, publication, and participation in national forums.

- Metrics to assess the progress of Physician Well-Being & Engagement have been developed and are routinely tracked across the company.

The End of the Beginning

President Barack Obama has signed the health reform bill (HR 3590-The Health & Student Loan Reconciliation Act) into law. The law requires all Americans to have health insurance and expands Medicaid eligibility for low-income adults and families. It remains unclear how this law, with individual and business mandates, insurance reform, and alterations to Medicaid and Medicare, will impact physicians. However, it is clear that existing and planned changes to governmental regulation and professional reimbursement are creating concern among physicians and motivating many who currently practice in the private sector to consider institutional employment.

The health care industry is on the cusp of significant change, propelled by business, government, technology, and societal expectations. There is little doubt that physician-hospital relationships must evolve to accommodate new realities. While we have only made a start in understanding and implementing this program, it is our belief that the concepts and practices of Physician Well-Being & Engagement will serve physicians and hospitals well and contribute to health and healing of our patients.

Upon his retirement from medical practice, Dr. Jack (the inspiring pediatric physician we met in section two) received a letter from Sally O'Neal, the mother of one of his patients. "What greater gift," the letter read, "than for our children to have grown up with Dr. Jack in their lives…You were always teaching, always preaching—family, love, prayer, faith, and social justice. You gave them your medical expertise, you comforted them, but most of all, you loved them."

Simply put, that's our goal, for our patients and for our doctors—medical expertise, wrapped up in comfort and delivered with love.

RESOURCE A: MISSION PEER REVIEW

Primary Areas of Emphasis:

1. Mission Overview

Most significant mission-related success past three years

Most significant current mission-related challenge

Unique program with greatest potential for replication

Future areas of focus for mission development

2. Leadership & Culture

Mission Focus

Personal Spirituality

Culture of Prayer & Worship

Pastoral Care

Inclusivity

Adventist Christian Identity

Vital Sign Metrics:

Mission Event Calendar

Patient Contact Metric

Inclusivity Graphic

3. Environment of Care

Employee Engagement

Patient & Family Loyalty

Physician Well-Being & Engagement

Service Orientation

Facility & Symbolism

Business Processes

Employee Engagement Score

Patient Satisfaction Score

Physician Engagement Score

4. Community Health

Ministry to Underserved

Community Engagement

Community Responsiveness

Civic & Spiritual Leader Perspectives

International Mission Outreach

Publications/Media

Community Health Financial Metric

List of Community Leadership Roles

Philanthropy & Volunteer Metrics

RESOURCE B: PHYSICIAN WELL-BEING & ENGAGEMENT COMMITTEE

COMPOSITION

The Physician Well-Being & Engagement Committee (PWEC) shall be a standing committee of the Hospital and shall consist of the designated Chairperson, the Chief Medical Officer, and five to seven physicians chosen by the Chairperson. Hospital members shall include the CEO, the COO, and the Director of Pastoral Care. The Director of Medical Staff Services shall designate staff support for the committee. The Chairperson of PWEC shall be appointed by the Hospital CEO.

DUTIES

The duties of the PWEC shall be:

1. Provide emphasis on physician well-being and engagement within the medical staff and hospital.
2. Develop and submit annual Plan for Physician Well-Being & Engagement.
3. Organize, support and promote initiatives in fulfillment of annual Plan.
4. Support the mission of the Hospital through physician engagement.

MEETINGS, REPORTS, RECOMMENDATIONS

The PWEC shall meet every other month and as needed to accomplish goals and transact business. The Office of Medical Staff Services shall maintain meeting reports and minutes. Copies of all minutes and reports shall be routinely forwarded to the CEO as prepared.

The Chairperson shall be available to meet with the CEO and/or the President of the Medical Staff as needed.

The presence of one-third of the total membership of the committee PWEC shall constitute a quorum, sufficient that the meeting may be conducted and business transacted.

Organizational Chart

Physician Well-Being & Engagement Committee

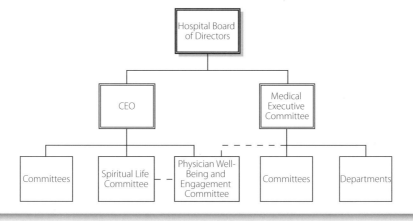

RESOURCE C: JOB DESCRIPTION: PWE COMMITTEE CHAIRPERSON

General Hospital
Position Description
Chairperson, Committee on Physician Well-Being & Engagement

REPORTING
The Committee Chair for Physician Well-Being & Engagement (PWE) reports directly to the Chief Executive Officer (CEO).

POSITION PURPOSE
The Committee Chair provides leadership and guidance to the medical staff and the PWE Committee and promotes effective communication among the medical staff, MEC, administration, and the Board.
This individual is responsible for:

1. Building relationships with colleagues on the medical staff.
2. Assessing medical staff status relative to engagement with the mission of the hospital.
3. Collaborating with clinical staff, pastoral care staff, administration and others to promote whole person care in the hospital.
4. Collaborating with senior hospital leadership to identify, support, and develop spiritual leaders within the medical staff.
5. Developing initiatives to support physicians in the pursuit of meaning, purpose, and balance in the practice of medicine.

ACCOUNTABILITY AND FUNCTIONS:
As required by his/her office, the Chair, PWE Committee must:

1. Act as Chair, PWE Committee, in coordination and cooperation with the CEO, CMO, and Senior Medical Staff Officers in matters of mutual concern involving the hospital and medical staff.
2. Call, preside at, and develop agenda for all regular and special meetings of the Physician Well-Being & Engagement Committee.
3. Provide leadership in the development of an Annual Plan for PWE.
4. Represent PWE Committee as a member of Medical Executive Committee.
5. Serve as liaison with Adventist Health System (AHS) Medical Mission Department.
6. Represent hospital on Adventist Health System PWE Council.
7. Participate in regular meetings of AHS PWE Council.
8. Support and promote PWE initiatives in fulfillment of annual PWE Plan.
9. Obtain necessary training to fulfill assigned responsibilities.
10. Consult with CMO and President of the Medical Staff on matters of special concern relative to health and balance among members of medical staff.
11. Serve as member of the Spiritual Life Advisory Committee of the hospital.
12. Collaborate with Pastoral Care Department to support spiritual interests of the medical staff.

13. Perform all functions as may be authorized in applicable policies.
14. Interacts and communicates on a regular basis with Medical Staff Departmental and Committee Chairs.
15. Attends all medical staff leadership development programs of the hospital.

POSITION REQUIREMENTS

1. Education
   Hold an MD or DO degree

2. Licensure
   Hold Board Certification in practicing specialty

3. Experience
   Active member of the medical staff in good standing for at least three years.
   Demonstrates commitment to the mission of the hospital.
   Demonstrates commitment to purpose, meaning, and balance in personal and professional life.
   Possesses familiarity with clinical care in the hospital setting.
   Medical staff leadership experience desirable (e.g. department or committee chair or higher).
   Be knowledgeable concerning duties described in this document and as outlined in medical staff bylaws.
   Possess extraordinary communication and relationship building skills.

4. Must use this hospital as primary hospital as determined by MEC.

5. Be willing to disclose and execute a Conflict of Interest Disclosure Statement listing all financial and conflicting interests.

6. Serve a term of two years.

ANTICIPATED TIME COMMITMENT

This position requires approximately eight (8) hours a month on leadership responsibilities.

RECOGNITION AND BENEFITS

The Chair of the Committee on Physician Health and Spirituality receives the following yearly benefit package:

- A stipend in the amount determined by the CEO, Governing Board, and MEC.
- Participation in the AHS Mission Conference.
- Participation in the AHS Physician Well-Being & Engagement Council.
- Administrative suport through the Medical Staff Services Office for correspondence, research, scheduling of meetings, and other clerical support as related to the position outlined in this job description.

ANTICIPATED POSITION CHALLENGES

The Chair of the PH&S Committee should anticipate some degree of challenge communicating the philosophy and concept of this position to medical colleagues.

PERFORMANCE EVALUATION

Annual performance evaluation shall be conducted at the discretion of the CEO and Medical Executive Committee.

RESOURCE D: LETTER OF AGREEMENT, PWE COMMITTEE CHAIRPERSON

January 1, 2050

LETTER OF AGREEMENT

Dear Doctor _____:

This letter will memorialize the terms of the Agreement between you and Name of Hospital (the "Hospital") relative to the performance of your duties as Chairperson, Physician Well-Being & Engagement Committee, for the two-year term beginning on April 1, 2006 and ending on March 31, 2008.

You will perform the duties of your office as outlined in, and in accordance with, the Medical Staff Bylaws and related documents to the best of your ability. Those duties have been summarized in the Position Description that is attached to this Agreement. You will devote such time to these duties as is reasonably necessary to fulfill your duties and responsibilities as Chairperson of the Committee.

Compensation: The Hospital will pay you Number thousand Dollars ($00,000) per year for the services that you provide to the Hospital as the Chairperson, Physician Well-Being & Engagement Committee. This Number thousand Dollars ($00,000) annual stipend will be paid in four (4) quarterly installments of Number thousand Dollars ($0,000) each. Each payment will be made at the end of the last month of the quarter in which the services were provided. You will be covered by the Hospital's Director's and Officer's liability insurance relative to the performance of your duties and will be provided with the other legal protections that are summarized in the attached Position Description.

Education: Physician shall be available to attend one or more educational seminars annually as may reasonably be requested by the Hospital. Seminars shall have as their purpose to teach both new and experienced physician-leaders skills and provide information that will assist them in succeeding in his/her medical staff leadership role. Upon receipt of proper documentation from the Physician, the Hospital shall authorize payment for reasonable tuition, travel and lodging expenses associated with attending seminars recommended and/or approved by the Hospital. Hours spent by the Physician in traveling to and from and attending educational programs pursuant to this paragraph shall be a cost borne by the Physician and shall not be compensated pursuant to the Agreement.

You will be considered an independent contractor and the Hospital will not withhold any taxes or other payments from the stipend and you will be responsible for paying the same.

The Hospital may terminate this Agreement and the payments hereunder prior to its expiration date if you:

1. Cease to be appointed to the professional staff; or

2. Are removed from your position of Chairperson; or

3. For failure to perform the duties of your office to the reasonable satisfaction of the Board of Trustees.

In the event of termination, your compensation will be prorated based upon the number of months actually served in the capacity of Chairperson.

Sincerely,

Attachment: Position Description _____

_____

_____

_____

I accept the above terms and agree to be legally bound hereby.

Date: _____

Signature: _____

RESOURCE E: Physician Recognition Award Documentation

FLORIDA HOSPITAL - 2009
VALUES AWARDS FOR PHYSICIANS ON THE MEDICAL STAFF
NOMINATING FORM

Also available on-line: **www.floridahospitalmd.org / Medical Staff /
2009 Physician Value Awards – Nomination Form**

Each year Florida Hospital presents Values Awards to those physicians deemed outstanding in fulfilling our mission and values in their professional and personal lives. Physicians from all Florida Hospital campuses are eligible for nomination. Nominations may be submitted by Florida Hospital leadership, employees, allied health professionals, and physician members of the medical staff. Use a separate form or sheet for each physician nominated.

Your nomination must reach your Campus Medical Staff Coordinator or Campus Executive Office by September 25, 2009 for consideration. Please **print legibly or type** your nomination information.

Name of Physician Nominee: _____
Physician's Specialty: _____
_____

Check only one Value per physician - (see corresponding criteria definitions)

_____ INTEGRITY		_____ EXCELLENCE
_____ COMPASSION		_____ STEWARDSHIP
_____ BALANCE		_____ TEAMWORK

Explain how the physician meets the criteria for the Value and went beyond that which is normally expected:

_____
_____

Submitted by: (Please include name, department, and campus. If needed, use additional page)

_____
_____

FLORIDA HOSPITAL
PHYSICIAN VALUES AWARDS CRITERIA
MEDICAL STAFF

I. INTEGRITY

Nominees for the Florida Hospital Integrity Award show extraordinary service to Florida Hospital beyond their everyday responsibilities. They demonstrate integrity by:

- Preserving other's dignity and maintaining confidentiality while communicating honestly with patients, their families and other healthcare professionals
- Earning the trust and respect of their patients and other healthcare professionals
- Living the "mission" of Florida Hospital by faithfully carrying out and going beyond their day to day medical staff responsibilities

This award may be given in honor of a unique circumstance, such as a sacrificial service in an emergency or the overcoming of personal adversity.

II. COMPASSION

Nominees for the Florida Hospital Compassion Award demonstrate personal values that inspire a physician to place the service of others above themselves and to treat others as they would want to be treated. They demonstrate compassion by:

- Demonstrating care and concern for others
- Demonstrating Florida Hospital SHARE principles in action
- Attentiveness to the detailed needs of patients, families and other healthcare professionals

III. BALANCE

The Balance Award recognizes those physicians who have embraced the concept that living harmoniously helps restore persons to the wholeness originally created by God. Accordingly, they have incorporated the practice of wholeness and harmony in body, mind and spirit in their personal lives. These physicians recognize that health is more than the absence of disease, and choose to maintain balance in their lives by dynamically focusing on the internal (mental, spiritual, emotional, physical) and external (family, job, community church) aspects of their lives.

IV. EXCELLENCE

The Excellence Award recognizes those physicians who embrace a philosophy of excellence in the area of physician development, clinical quality, patient satisfaction, clinical research for the betterment of those we serve, and/or outstanding achievement in the nominee's professional arena. The achievement of excellence in the areas noted above must be of outstanding and notable prominence.

V. STEWARDSHIP

The Stewardship Award recognizes those physicians who have embraced a challenge and succeeded in improving patient care, while reducing costs eliminating rework, or simplifying the work processes. Nominees for the Stewardship Award include those physicians who have used the principles of Continuous Quality Improvement to achieve measurable improvement. New programs, new procedures, or other changes that improve Florida Hospital are the hallmarks of the Stewardship Award.

VI. TEAMWORK

Nominees for the Florida Hospital Teamwork Award demonstrate personal values that inspire a physician to place a collaborative spirit toward a common goal above individual needs

and desires. They demonstrate teamwork by:
- Active participation in multi-disciplinary teams or meetings
- Taking on assignments, responsibilities for encouraging other physician's participation
- Effectively communicating issues and working toward resolution of issues

FH VALUE AWARDS: SELECTION PROCESS FOR 2009

CIRCULATION:
- Memo to Division Chiefs and Assistant Chiefs of Staff, Division Secretary/Treasurers, Medical Staff Coordinators, Campus Administrators, Assistant Campus Administrators, and Chief Nursing Officers
- Nomination Form and Value Criteria included with above memo
- Other suggestions:
    1. Email to campus personnel responsible for distribution
    2. Campus employee newsletter
    3. FH TV (Medical Staff Services is checking to see if possible)
    4. All Medical Staff and Allied Health professionals (Medical Staff Services will send via email and fax)

NOMINATIONS:
- Nominations gathered at the campuses
- Campus reviews and selects only those nominees deemed to be eligible for the award – per the memo
- Nominees selected and submitted to Janice Stephens in Medical Staff Services by Friday, October 9, 2009

SELECTION:
- Upon return to the Medical Staff Services Office, nominations to be grouped by Division and copied by color code
- Nominations will be provided to the Selection Committee for their review prior to convening, along with names of previous recipients, and cover memo
- Selection Committee to meet to make final selections and choose one physician for each of the six Values: Integrity / Compassion / Balance / Excellence / Stewardship / Teamwork
- Selection Committee composed of:

Chief Medical Officer	VP, Physician Strategic Development
President, Medical Staff	Immediate Past President, Medical Staff
Secretary/Treasurer, Medical Staff	President Elect, Medical Staff
Senior Patient Care Officer	Director, Medical Staff Services

NOTIFICATION
- Individuals chosen will be personally notified by Janice Stephens that they have been selected to receive the value award.
- Once notified, names will be provided to the videography team to schedule appointment for filming and videography.

RESOURCE F: PHYSICIAN ORIENTATION SAMPLE TEMPLATE

**Hospital Physician Orientation
Sample Template – Adventist Health System**

	Responsible	Source	Date
1. Organization & Facility	**CEO**		
Corporate:			
Adventist Health System		**Video**	
Mission, Vision, Values		**Video**	
Annual Report		**Document**	
Hospital:	**CEO**		
History and Heritage		**Video**	
Clinical and Ancillary Services		**Brochure**	
Community Role		**Discussion**	
Hospital Tour & Introductions:	**COO/CNO**		
Administration			
Organizational Chart		**Document**	
Hospital Phone Directory		**Document**	
Pastoral Care	**Chaplain**	**Visit**	
Medical Staff Office	**CMO/MS Sec'y**		
Application/Privileges		**Document**	
Medical Staff Directory		**Document**	
Meeting Schedule		**Document**	
Personal Contact Information		**Distribution**	
Bylaws, Rules & Regs		**Document**	
Code of Conduct P&P		**Document**	
Call Schedule		**Document**	
Medical Staff President		**Introduction**	
Departmental Chairperson		**Introduction**	
Parking		**Card**	
Building Access		**Card/Key**	
Physician Lounge			
Food Service			
Emergency Department			
Surgical Suite			
2. Processes & Procedures			
MIS Access and Tools:	**Dir, MIS**		
iConnect			
CPOE			
PACS			
Dictation			
Hospital ID #			

	Responsible	Source	Date
Physician Orders		Med Records	
Medical Records		Med Records	
Hospitalist Availability & Role		Introduction	
Regulatory Considerations:	Dir, QA		
Joint Commission			
Corporate Compliance			
HIPAA			
Quality and Utilization:	Dir, QA		
Patient Safety and Quality Initiatives			
Case Management			
Discharge Planning			
3. **Practice Orientation** (Employed Physicians)	Prac Mgr		
Medical License			
DEA License			
Medicare/Medicaid Application			
HMO/PPO Provider Application(s)			
Community Announcements			
Practice Tour			
Human Resources Coordination			
Office Furnishings			
Coding & Billing Training			
Letterhead/Business Cards			
Vacation Scheduling Process			
Employment Application			

RESOURCE G: SEMINAR TOPICS AND SPEAKERS

Calling Out the Best in Medicine: An Antidote for Challenging Times, Penny Williamson, ScD

The Courage to Lead, Penny Williamson, ScD and Herdley O. Paolini, PhD

Relational Health of the Physician and Its' Impact on Patient Care, Dr. Alan Nelson

Physician Relationships with Patients, Staff and Colleagues and Their Impact on Patient, Dr. Alan Nelson

Spirituality and Medicine: Latest Research and Clinical Applications, Harold C. Koenig, MD

Medicine in the 21st Century: Reconciling Physical and Spiritual Healing Dale A. Matthews, MD, FACP

Communication: Keys to Successful Leadership, Rufus Barfield, PhD and Herdley Paolini, PhD

The Heart of Medicine: Relationships, Herdley O Paolini, PhD

Singular Intimacies: Literature as a Bridge Between Doctor & Patient, Danielle Ofri, MD, PhD

Domestic Violence, Herdley O. Paolini, PhD

HIV, Michael Gebel, MD

Prevention of Medical Errors, Joseph Portoghese, MD

Spirit in Medicine, Malcolm Herring, MD; Herdley O. Paolini, PhD & Shawn Zimmerman, PhD

Smoking Cessation: Building a Foundation for Proactive Health, Frederic Seifer, MD

Motivational Interviewing, Herdley O. Paolini, PhD and Timothy Spruill, EdD

Physician Life Meaning & Its Impact on Patient Care and Outcomes, Shawn Zimmerman, PhD

Physicians and Relationships of Significance, Herdley O. Paolini, PhD

Navigating Medical Practice in an Emotionally Intelligent Way, Shawn Zimmerman, PhD

The Interrelationship of Science and Soul: Models for Navigating Medical Practice, Christina Puchalski, MD, MS

Physician Communication and Leadership Development, Faith Evans

The Art and Science of Meaning and Its Implications for Medical Practice, Herdley Paolini, PhD, Shawn Zimmerman, PhD, Timothy Spruill, EdD

Remembering Our Power to Make a Difference, Rachael Naomi Remen, MD;

Gifted Hands-The Art of Daily Practice, Ben Carson, MD

Creating Your Own Future-Leadership as Antidote Against Victimization, Kenneth Cohn, MD, MBA, FACS; Thomas Werner, President Emeritus.

RESOURCE H: LIBRARY SUGGESTED VOLUMES

BOOK SELECTIONS
PHYSICIAN WELL-BEING & SPIRITUALITY

A Piece of My Mind: Essays and Letters from the Journal of the American Medical Association. Feeling Fine Programs, Inc., and Alfred A Knopf, Inc., 1988.

Healing the Wounds: A Physician Looks at His Work. Hilfiker MD, David. Pantheon Books, New York, 1985.

Incidental Findings: Lessons from My Patients in the Art of Medicine. Ofri MD, Danielle. Beacon Press, Boston, 2005.

The Science of Optimism and Hope: Research Essays in Honor of Martin E. P. Seligman. Templeton Foundation Press, 2000.

Spirituality in Patient Care: Why, How, When, and What. Koenig MD, Harold G. Templeton Foundation Press, 2002. *(Also numerous other titles by Dr. Koenig)*

When Sickness Heals: The Place of Religious Belief in Healthcare. Sorajjakool, Siroj. Templeton Foundation Press, 2006.

The Healer's Calling: A spirituality for physicians and other health care professionals. Sulmasy MD, Daniel P. Paulist Press, 1997.

A Balm for Gilead: Meditations on spirituality and the healing arts. Sulmasy MD, Daniel P. Georgetown University Press, 2006.

The Faith Factor: Proof of the healing power of prayer. Matthews MD, Dale. Penguin Books, 1998.

A Thousand Miracles Every Day: A selection of stories that shaped the mission and history of Adventist hospitals. Quevedo, Jane Allen. TEACH Services, Inc., 2003.

Agape Love: A tradition found in eight world religions. Sir John Templeton. Templeton Foundation Press, 1999.

Tracks of a Fellow Struggler: Living and growing through grief. Claypool, John R. Morehouse Publishing, 2004.

The Handbook of Physician Health: The essential guide to understanding the health needs of physicians. Edited by Larry S. Goldman, MD; Michael Myers, MD; Leah J. Dickstein, MD. American Medical Association, 2000.

The Soul of the Physician: Doctors speaking about passion, resilience, and hope. Linda G. Henry and James D. Henry. American Medical Association, 2002.

The Resilient Physician: Effective emotional management for doctors and their medical organizations. Wayne M. Sotile and Mary O. Sotile. American Medical Association, 2002.

RESOURCE I: Department of Healthcare & Spirituality

**MEDICAL STAFF ORGANIZATIONAL MANUAL – ARTICLE IV
MEDICAL STAFF COMMITTEES AND FUNCTIONS**

PART I: DEPARTMENT OF HEALTHCARE & SPIRITUALITY

Section 1.   Organization:

The attainment of the department's goals and objectives shall be physician driven with administrative support.

The chairman of the Department of Healthcare & Spirituality shall be appointed by the President of the Medical Staff and endorsed by the Medical Executive Committee.

PART I:

Section 2.   Goals and Objectives:

(a) Educate and facilitate physician understanding on the spiritual aspects of patient care.

(b) Collaborate with the healthcare delivery team on the spiritual aspects of patient care with emphasis and consultation from the Pastoral Care team.

(c) Collaborate and further establish relationships with faith communities and their leaders on the spiritual care of patients.

(d) Support and foster the spiritual life and wellbeing of physicians.

(e) Identify Florida Hospital's and national best practices and collect data to determine where evidence supports improved outcomes.

PART I:

Section 3.   Meetings, Reports and Recommendations:

A yearly report shall be provided to the Executive Committee to review the goals, objectives, and outcomes of the program.

PART I:

Section 4.   Division Sections:

(a) Composition:
The division sections of the Department of Healthcare and Spirituality shall consist of the Senior Campus Administrator, the Division Chief of Staff, or his/her designee, the Head Chaplain at the division, and the Division Chief Nursing Officer, or his/her designee, and any division member who wishes to participate.

(b) Meetings, Reports and Recommendations:
It is recommended that the Division Healthcare and Spirituality sections meet on a monthly basis. Any reports or recommendations shall be forwarded to the Division Quarterly Healthcare and Spirituality meetings.

NOTES

1. Steiger, Bill. "Survey Results: Doctors Say Morale is Hurting." *The Physician Executive*, Nov-Dec 2006, 6-15.

2. Sulmasy OFM, MD, Daniel. *The Healer's Calling: A Spirituality for Physicians and other Health Care Professionals*, Paulist Press, 1997, pg 8.

3. Howard, Chris. "Restructuring Hospital-Physician Relationships for Future Success." *Frontiers of Health Service Management* 20:2, 23-30.

4. Steiger, Bill. "Survey Results: Doctors Say Morale is Hurting." *The Physician Executive*, Nov Dec 2006, 6-15.

5. Shanafelt, Tait D., et al. "The Well-Being of Physicians." *The American Journal of Medicine* 114 (April 15, 2003): 513-19.

6. Schernhammer, MD "Taking Their Own Lives—The High Rate of Physician Suicide." New *England Journal of Medicine* 352, no. 24 (June 16, 2005): 2473-2476.

7. Bujak MD, Joseph S. "How to Improve Hospital-Physician Relationships," *Frontiers of Health Service Management* 20, no.2: 3-21.

8. Pellegrino E., MD. "Educating the Christian Physician: Being Christian and Being a Physician". Hospital Progress 1979 Aug; 60 (8):46-53.

9. Fox, Zeni and Bechtle, Regina. *Called & Chosen: Toward a Spirituality for Lay Leaders*. Lanham, MD: Roman & Littlefield, 2005.

10. Kaplan, Marty. "Ambushed by Spirituality." *Time*, June 24, 1996, 62.

11. Curlin, Farr, et al. "Religious Characteristics of U. S. Physicians." *Journal of General Internal Medicine* 20 (2005): 629-634.

12. Bujak MD, Joseph S. "How to Improve Hospital-Physician Relationships," *Frontiers of Health Service Management* 20, no.2: 3-21.

13. Bogue, Richard, et al. "Secrets of Physician Satisfaction." *The Physician Executive*, Nov-Dec 2006, 30-37.

14. Herring MD, Malcolm B and Rahman MD, Jon D. "Physicians and Spirituality." *Health Progress*, July-Aug 2004.

15. Toto, Deborah. "What the Doctor Ordered." *Gallup Management Journal*, Sept 8, 2005.

16. Rice, Richard. *Ministryhealing: Toward a Theology of Wholeness and Witness*. Loma Linda, CA: Loma Linda University Press, 2006.

17. Pellegrino E., MD. "Educating the Christian Physician: Being Christian and Being a Physician". Hospital Progress 1979 Aug; 60 (8):46-53.

18. Wallace LS, Cassada DC, Ergen WF, Goldman MH. "Setting the stage: Surgery patients' expectations for greetings during routine office visits." *Journal of Surgical Research* 157, no. 1 (Nov. 2009): 91-5

19. The Joint Commission. "Behaviors that Undermine a Culture of Safety." *Sentinel Event Alert* 40 (July 9, 2008).

20. Johnson, Carrie. "Bad Blood: Doctor-Nurse Behavior Problems Impact Patient Care." *The Physician Executive Journal of Medical Management* 35, no.6 (Nov-Dec 2009): 6-11.

21. The Joint Commission. "Behaviors that Undermine a Culture of Safety." *Sentinel Event Alert* 40 (July 9, 2008).

22. Cohn KH, Gill SL, and Schwartz RW. "Gaining Hospital Administrator's Attention: Ways to Improve Physician-Hospital Management Dialogue." *Surgery* 137 (2005): 132-40.

23. Bujak MD, Joseph S. "How to Improve Hospital-Physician Relationships," *Frontiers of Health Service Management* 20, no.2: 3-21.

24. *Guide to Good Medical Practice*—USA. Version 1.1, March 9, 2009, pg. 3. Developed by the National Alliance for Physician Competence.

25. Billiar TR. "Presidential address: Routine Complexity." *Surgery* 130 (2001): 123-32.

26. Reinertsen JL, Gosfield AG, Rupp W, Whittington JW. *Engaging Physicians in a Shared Quality Agenda*. IHI Innovation Series White Paper, Cambridge, MA: Institute for Healthcare Improvement, 2007, www.IHI.org.

27. Ortolon, Ken. "God, MD: Medicine Rediscovers the Role of Spirituality in Health Care." *Texas Medicine*, November 2004, 40-42.

28. Kaplan, Marty. "Ambushed by Spirituality." *Time*, June 24, 1996, 62.

29. Tanner, Lindsey. Associated Press Wire Service, June 27, 2005.

30. Koenig, Harold MD. "Religion, Spirituality, and Medicine: Research Findings and Implications for Clinical Practice." *Southern Medical Journal* 97, no. 12 (Dec 2004): 1194-1200.

31. Anandarajah, Gowri MD. "The 3 H and BMSEST Models for Spirituality in Multicultural Whole-Person Medicine." *Annals of Family Medicine* 6, no. 5 (Sept-Oct 2008): 448-458.

32. Koenig, Harold MD. "Religion, Spirituality, and Medicine: Research Findings and Implications for Clinical Practice." *Southern Medical Journal* 97, no. 12 (Dec 2004): 1194-1200.

33. Sulmasy OFM, MD, Daniel. *The Healer's Calling: A Spirituality for Physicians and other Health Care Professionals*, Paulist Press, 1997, pg 61-62.

ACKNOWLEDGEMENTS

I WOULD LIKE TO THANK Tom Werner, former President and CEO of Adventist Health System (AHS), who envisioned and initiated the Physician Well-Being & Engagement effort that provides the basis for this monograph.

Donald Jernigan, current AHS President and CEO, provided unflagging encouragement and executive leadership as the program has developed and grown. Terry Shaw, AHS CFO, enabled this work through financial counsel and support.

Trail blazers and early adopters from whose thinking, creativity, and zeal we have benefited include Harold Koenig, Dan Sulmasy, Malcolm Herring, Herdley Paolini, Ken Bradley, John Guarneri, Richard Bogue, Jeff Wood, Steven Jeffers, Karen Schefter, and Terri Schultz.

Physician leaders who embraced this effort and supported it with time, energy, enthusiasm and expertise include Loran Hauck, Doug Bechard, Phil Smith, Terry O'Rourke, Dianne McCallister, Peter Edelstein, Fred Myers, and Ron Jimenez.

This is work that is essentially spiritual in nature, touching upon the heart and soul of medical life and practice. Many pastoral care leaders have contributed to this work through wise counsel and engagement with physicians in the clinical setting. These include Sister Nancy Hoffman, John Rapp, Stephen King, Peter Bath, Greg Ellis, Jay Perez, Faye Rose, and Jaime Guajardo.

Special thanks to those who generously gave of their time and expertise to review the manuscript and provide gracious and candid feedback, including Randy Haffner, Joyce Portela, Malcolm Herring, Herdley Paolini, Brian Yanofchick, and Doug Bechard.

This work owes much to the patience and technical support of my assistant, Janet Griffin and to Cason Jones at the Florida Hospital Medical Library for her assistance in the extensive research conducted for this publication. Todd Chobotar's editorial guidance, encouragement, and direction made it possible, and Lillian Boyd tied it all together. I'm also grateful for Stephanie Lind's marketing wisdom and guidance.

My last and best thank you to my wife, Jackie, and our wonderful family for contributing so much to my "well-being and engagement" over a busy forty-year career of education, practice, administration, and, finally, the development of this program and production of this book.

ABOUT THE AUTHOR

THE SIGN IS MADE of black plexiglas with raised white letters, framed in rich red oak. Twelve inches high by 30 inches wide, it reads: *Ted Hamilton, MD, Family Practice.*

Dr. Hamilton hung that "shingle" at the entrance to his office in the rural mountains of western North Carolina in June, 1974. Five years and more than five hundred babies later, he left the mountains to teach family medicine to aspiring young residents at Florida Hospital in Orlando. It was there that he discovered an aptitude for medical administration that led him to complete a master's degree in business and to pursue a career in physician leadership.

Dr. Hamilton has wide experience in medical practice and administration, having worked as executive director for a large academic physician practice plan affiliated with Loma Linda University School of Medicine; medical director for HMO Georgia, a division of Blue Cross and Blue Shield; Chief Medical Officer of Florida Hospital, an eight-campus, 2,000-bed institution; and as medical consultant to Tennessee's Medicaid program. Along the way, Dr. Hamilton continued part-time clinical work in various acute care settings.

Community service has been an important part of Dr. Hamilton's life. He volunteered and served as a board member for organizations providing healthcare services for the homeless and uninsured. Other significant community interests include blood procurement and food provision for the hungry. He is an adjunct professor, having taught graduate-level courses in Healthcare Policy and Administration.

Married, with two daughters and two grandchildren, Dr. Hamilton is active in his local church and enjoys water sports, golf, snow-skiing, and is an avid reader.

FLORIDA HOSPITAL

The skill to heal. The spirit to care.

Florida Hospital Celebration Health

Florida Hospital Altamonte

GINSBURG

Florida Hospital Winter Park

Florida Hospital Orlando

Florida Hospital East Orlando

Florida Hospital Apopka

Florida Hospital Kissimmee

ABOUT FLORIDA HOSPITAL

For over one hundred years the mission of Florida Hospital has been: *To extend the health and healing ministry of Christ.* Opened in 1908, Florida Hospital is comprised of seven hospital campuses housing over 2,000 beds and eighteen walk-in medical centers. With over 16,000 employees—including 2,000 doctors and 4,000 nurses—Florida Hospital serves the residents and guests of Orlando, the No. 1 tourist destination in the world. Florida Hospital cares for over one million patients a year. Florida Hospital is a Christian, faith-based hospital that believes in providing Whole Person Care to all patients – mind, body and spirit. Hospital fast facts include:

- **LARGEST ADMITTING HOSPITAL IN AMERICA.** Ranked No. 1 in the nation for inpatient admissions by the *American Hospital Association*.

- **AMERICA'S HEART HOSPITAL.** Ranked No. 1 in the nation for number of heart procedures performed each year, averaging 15,000 cases annually. MSNBC named Florida Hospital "America's Heart Hospital" for being the No. 1 hospital fighting America's No. 1 killer—heart disease.

- **HOSPITAL OF THE FUTURE.** At the turn of the century, the *Wall Street Journal* named Florida Hospital the "Hospital of the Future".

- **ONE OF AMERICA'S BEST HOSPITALS.** Recognized by *U.S. News & World Report* as "One of America's Best Hospitals" for ten years. Clinical specialties recognized have included: Cardiology, Orthopaedics, Neurology & Neurosurgery, Urology, Gynecology, Digestive Disorders, Hormonal Disorders, Kidney Disease, Ear, Nose & Throat and Endocrinology.

- **LEADER IN SENIOR CARE.** Florida Hospital serves the largest number of seniors in America through Medicare with a goal for each patient to experience a "Century of Health" by living to a healthy hundred.

- **TOP BIRTHING CENTER.** *Fit Pregnancy* magazine named Florida Hospital one of the "Top 10 Best Places in the Country to have a Baby". As a result, *The Discovery Health Channel* struck a three-year production deal with Florida Hospital to host a live broadcast called "Birth Day Live". Florida Hospital annually delivers over 9,000 babies.

- **CORPORATE ALLIANCES.** Florida Hospital maintains corporate alliance relationships with a select group of Fortune 500 companies including Disney, Nike, Johnson & Johnson, Philips, AGFA, and Stryker.

- **DISNEY PARTNERSHIP.** Florida Hospital is the Central Florida health & wellness resource of the *Walt Disney World* ® Resort. Florida Hospital also partnered with Disney to build the ground breaking health and wellness facility called Florida Hospital Celebration Health located in Disney's town of Celebration, Florida. Disney and Florida Hospital recently partnered to build a new state-of-the-art Children's Hospital.

- **HOSPITAL OF THE 21ST CENTURY.** Florida Hospital Celebration Health was awarded the *Premier Patient Services Innovator Award* as "The Model for Healthcare Delivery in the 21st Century".

- **SPORTS EXPERTS.** Florida Hospital is the official hospital of the Orlando *Magic* NBA basketball team. In addition, Florida Hospital has an enduring track record of providing exclusive medical care to many sports organizations. These organizations have included: Disney's Wide World of Sports, Walt Disney World's Marathon Weekend, the Capital One Bowl, and University of Central Florida Athletics. Florida Hospital has also provided comprehensive healthcare services for the World Cup and Olympics.

- **PRINT RECOGNITION.** Self magazine named Florida Hospital one of America's "Top 10 Hospitals for Women". *Modern Healthcare* magazine proclaimed it one of America's best hospitals for cardiac care.

- **CONSUMER CHOICE AWARD WINNER.** Florida Hospital has received the Consumer Choice Award from the *National Research Corporation* every year from 1996 to the present.

HEAR MORE FROM DR. TED HAMILTON

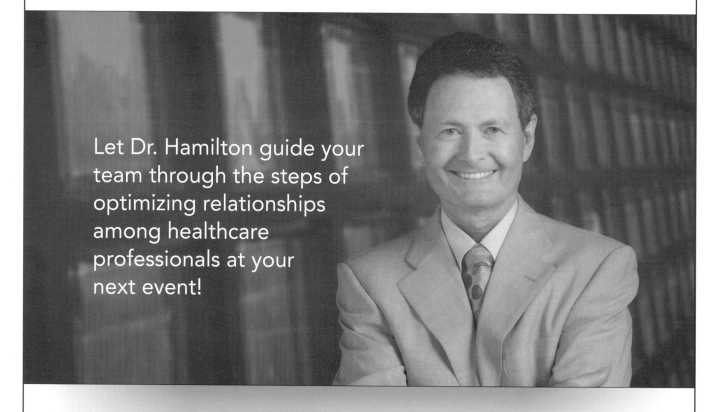

Let Dr. Hamilton guide your team through the steps of optimizing relationships among healthcare professionals at your next event!

DR. HAMILTON'S TOPICS:

- **Building Bridges: Optimizing Physician Well-Being & Engagement**

- **Physician-Nurse Collaboration: The Key to Outstanding Patient Care**

- **Patient Experience: What Patients Really Want and How to Make It Happen**

- **Corn, Coffee, Wheat, Doctor: Are We Mere Commodities in the Medical Marketplace?**

- **House Rules: Professional Behavior in the Hospital Setting**

- **Balancing Act: Walking the High Wire of Medical Practice Without Falling Off**

SPEAKING/CONSULTING – Have a topic you'd like to hear Dr. Ted Hamilton speak on that's not listed here? Simply fill out one of our Speaker Inquiry forms at FloridaHospitalPublishing.com, and we will work with you to customize a speech that is just right for your group. Or inquire about Dr. Hamilton's consulting availability to work directly with your leadership team.

ORLANDO SEMINARS – When you visit us online you can also reserve your seat at Dr. Hamilton's next seminar being taught in Orlando, Florida.

OTHER SPEAKERS – Need to schedule a speaker for your next conference, seminar or event? Florida Hospital Speakers Bureau can provide exactly what you need. Whether it's a keynote, a seminar, or a speech designed to fit your needs, we have a growing list of speakers dedicated to bringing you the latest in Healthcare and Leadership topics from a Whole Person Health perspective.

To book a speaker or register for a seminar, please visit:

www.FLORIDAHOSPITALPUBLISHING.com